# TRAGEDY AND BETRAYAL IN THE DUTCH RESISTANCE

*Dedicated to the women of the Meppelerstraatweg.*

*Motto: Don't forget us.*

# TRAGEDY AND BETRAYAL IN THE DUTCH RESISTANCE

SAMUEL DE KORTE

Pen & Sword
**MILITARY**
AN IMPRINT OF PEN & SWORD BOOKS LTD.
YORKSHIRE – PHILADELPHIA

Originally published in 2019 by Brave New Books as *Executie aan de Meppelerstraatweg: Zwolle 31 maart 1945*

First published in Great Britain in 2020 by
**PEN AND SWORD MILITARY**
An imprint of
Pen & Sword Books Limited
Yorkshire – Philadelphia

Copyright © Samuel de Korte, 2020

ISBN 978 1 52678 498 8

The right of Samuel de Korte to be identified as Author of this work has been asserted by him in accordance with the Copyright, Designs and Patents Act 1988.

A CIP catalogue record for this book is available from the British Library.

All rights reserved. No part of this book may be reproduced or transmitted in any form or by any means, electronic or mechanical including photocopying, recording or by any information storage and retrieval system, without permission from the Publisher in writing.

Typeset in Times New Roman 11.5/14 by
SJmagic DESIGN SERVICES, India.
Printed and bound in the UK by TJ Books, Padstow, Cornwall.

Pen & Sword Books Limited incorporates the imprints of Atlas, Archaeology, Aviation, Discovery, Family History, Fiction, History, Maritime, Military, Military Classics, Politics, Select, Transport, True Crime, Air World, Frontline Publishing, Leo Cooper, Remember When, Seaforth Publishing, The Praetorian Press, Wharncliffe Local History, Wharncliffe Transport, Wharncliffe True Crime and White Owl.

*For a complete list of Pen & Sword titles please contact*
**PEN & SWORD BOOKS LIMITED**
47 Church Street, Barnsley, South Yorkshire S70 2AS, United Kingdom
E-mail: enquiries@pen-and-sword.co.uk
Website: www.pen-and-sword.co.uk

Or
PEN AND SWORD BOOKS
1950 Lawrence Rd, Havertown, PA 19083, USA
E-mail: Uspen-and-sword@casematepublishers.com
Website: www.penandswordbooks.com

# Contents

|  |  |  |
|---|---|---|
| | Foreword | vi |
| | Map of The Netherlands | viii |
| | Introduction | ix |
| Chapter 1 | A Horrid Execution | 1 |
| Chapter 2 | The Five Men and Their Families | 3 |
| Chapter 3 | In the *Huis van Bewaring* | 55 |
| Chapter 4 | The Verdict and Westerbork | 72 |
| Chapter 5 | The Aftermath | 87 |
| Chapter 6 | Perpetrators and Collaborators | 98 |
| Chapter 7 | The Monument and Reflections | 113 |
| | Endnotes | 118 |
| | Abbreviations | 131 |
| | Bibliography | 132 |
| | Archives | 134 |
| | Family Sources | 135 |
| | Index | 136 |

# Foreword

In the Netherlands and elsewhere in Europe the Second World War is always close by. Everywhere there are monuments that commemorate the period of 1939/1940-1945. We pass these memorials while we are on our way to work, to school or the supermarket, or when we take a relaxing afternoon stroll or ride a bike. How often do we walk, cycle or drive by such a monument without paying attention to it? And even if we stop our everyday thoughts and briefly pause at the monument, do we know the dramatic story that hides behind it? No matter how magnificent or creatively they have been designed, they remain objects of stone, glass or metal, more capable of conveying emotion than a statement of fact.

Between the two lanes of the Meppelerstraatweg in the Dutch city of Zwolle is such a monument. The traffic roars by irreverently one hour after another, day by day. A simple, stone cross and five cut-off pillars, it's not very remarkable. At the slab there are five names recorded in black letters: H. Bosch, W.A. van Dijk, J.A. Muller, W. Sebel and B.J. IJzerman. '*Gefusilleerd 31 maart 1945*' (Shot 31 March 1945) is written above these names. On the basis of the given dates of birth and birthplace, we can conclude that the oldest victim would have been 55 on 24 May 1945, while the youngest was 31 on 5 January 1945. More cannot be deduced from the text on the plaque.

Every year on 31 March flowers and wreaths are placed at the monument, among others by children from a local school, so these names are not forgotten. Here five men are remembered who were executed in retaliation by the German occupiers just before the Liberation. The victims were captured on suspicion of anti-German activities and on that tragic day taken by their executioners to this place where a firing squad ended their lives. They were just five victims from the Nazi's many times larger total throughout the Netherlands; merely a footnote in the history of the German occupation, but an event that for the descendants of the victims must have seemed as if their world had collapsed.

# FOREWORD

One of these five men, Wilhelmus van Dijk, is a family member of the Dutch history student Samuel de Korte, the author of this book. He decided to look into the fate of Wilhelmus and the four others. Using the skills mastered during his studies, he researched archive material, spoke with descendants and finally wrote this book. Here he turns the five names into people of flesh and blood, men that went to school, worked, were mobilized in the Battle of the Netherlands in 1940, and, above all, had family lives. Their deaths left an emptiness in the lives of their loved ones. Thanks to this research they will not be forgotten, and their entire lives will not just be remembered as names on a monument.

Actually, everyone during the Second World War who was killed without a fair trial by the occupying forces deserves, besides a monument, a book like this.

Kevin Prenger

*Chief Editor Articles TracesOfWar.com*
*Stichting Informatie Wereldoorlog Twee (STIWOT)*

# TRAGEDY AND BETRAYAL IN THE DUTCH RESISTANCE

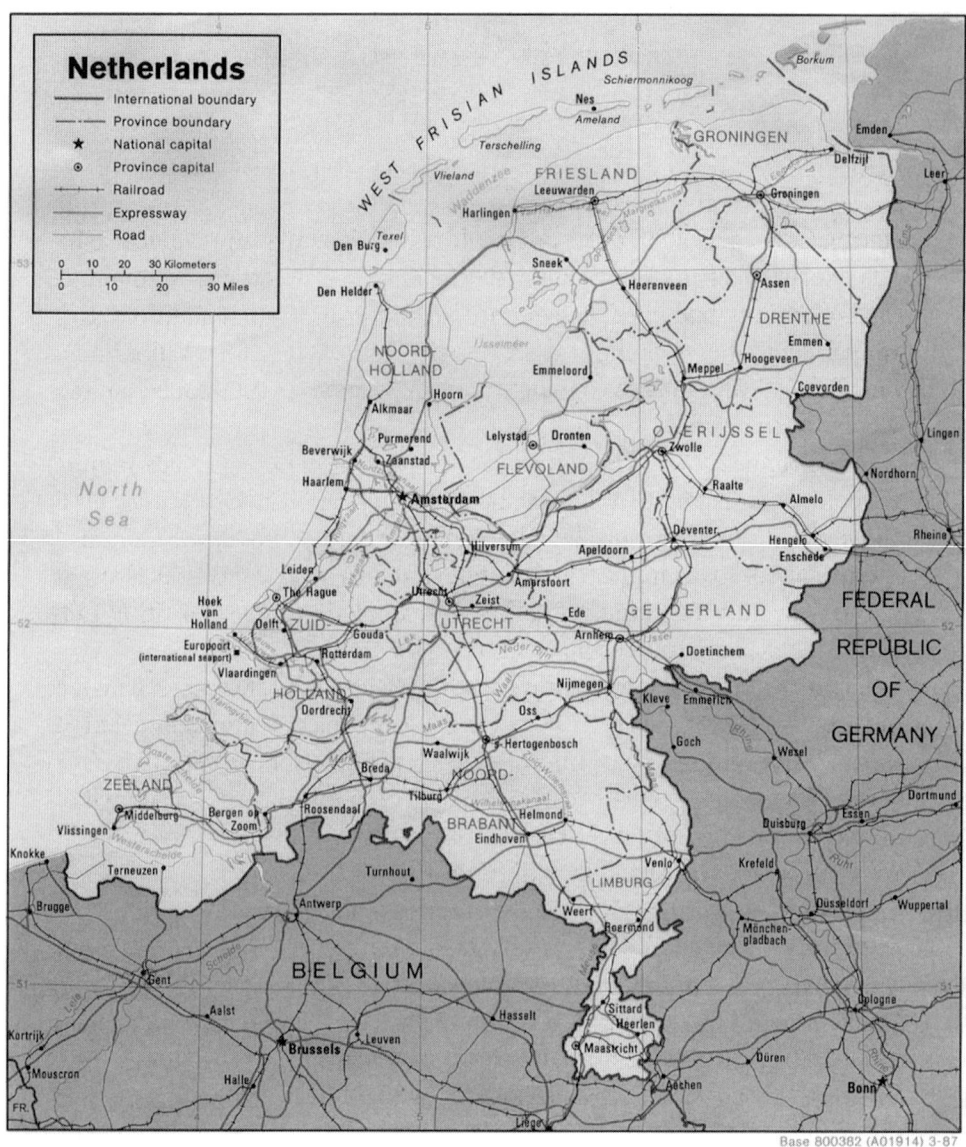

© Maps of Europe Viu Wikimedia Commons.

# Introduction

During Christmas 2017 my mother told me we had a family member who was executed during the Second World War. His name was Wilhelmus van Dijk and he had lived in Zwolle, a town approximately 80 kilometres away. He was the brother of my maternal great grandmother, Wilhelmina van Dijk. Wilhelmus was mentioned at a monument placed at the Meppelerstraatweg.

According to the stories that had been passed down in the family, Wilhelmus was part of the Resistance movement and had blown up a railway bridge. As a result, he and others were captured by the Germans and executed. I was immediately interested. The Resistance, the Second World War and blowing up a railway bridge! It sounded exciting and with enthusiasm I started the research.

There was some information available about the monument at the Meppelerstraatweg, as well as of the five men that died there, but it wasn't much. Another execution that took place in the vicinity two days before, on 29 March 1945 in Wierden, was the subject of a book, while the executions in Zwolle in April 1945 were dealt with in another book. For this reason, the focus is on the execution of 31 March 1945.

The reality turned out to be different than I assumed. Besides the previously mentioned story, I was also told that Wilhelmus van Dijk was betrayed by a jealous nurse who was in love with him. When he rejected her, she reported him to the German occupying forces to take revenge. Together with his wife, Hendrica Verhoeven, Wilhelmus van Dijk was transported to Westerbork, a local concentration camp. After spending some time there, he was transferred to Germany. When the vehicle was on the Meppelerstraatweg, Wilhelmus and several others tried to escape by jumping from the truck and were shot down. While it is, again, a fascinating story, it's not what happened in the early morning of 31 March 1945, and the story has been clouded by many retellings.

# TRAGEDY AND BETRAYAL IN THE DUTCH RESISTANCE

Wilhelmus van Dijk hadn't blown up the railway bridge. Others did that. He was not shot while trying to escape, but was lined up at the Meppelerstraatweg. He and the four others were shot during a reprisal, because other members of the Resistance had blown up the railway bridge. Because the truth turned out to be different than what I had been told, my aim has been to discover what really happened. Information about the five executed men wasn't easy to find, but I wanted to share what we have discovered. It's important to share knowledge and an article about the men and their lives would have been appropriate.

The research proceeded erratically, because new information became available, not only about the execution, but also about the men and what they had done. All of them were married, all of them had children. Their lives and their premature deaths left scars on the lives of their loved ones. Therefore, the suffering of their relatives will also have a place, in order to understand the sacrifice of the men better and to clarify the tragedy of the Second World War. The goal wasn't just to give meaning to the names on a monument, but to show the men and their lives up to the final moment.

The result is this book about the execution at the Meppelerstraatweg. It is my attempt to give them their place in history. Clearly written evidence was not always available, partially through the secretive nature of the Resistance, but also because there were plenty of stories. Members of the Resistance had to be private about their actions, as it was vital to their survival. The people that joined the Resistance early on only survived because they were so secretive.

I've had help from many sides for this book, including my family, my friends and people that gave me advice, regardless of whether I asked for it. Many others took the time to answer my questions. The list of people would be too long to mention all of them, however, I wish to acknowledge that without the staff of the Stadsarchief Kampen, the Oorlogsgravenstichting, the Nederlands Instituut voor Oorlogs-, Holocaust en Genocidestudies (NIOD), het Archief gemeente Hardenberg, the Nationaal Archief, the semi-statisch informatiebeheer van Defensie, the Historisch centrum Overijssel, this book wouldn't have existed. I also would like to thank the people at Pen & Sword, without them this translation would not have existed.

Besides that, several people lent me their memories and pictures including: Piet van Dijk, Ger van Dijk, Hillie van der Heijden-Sebel,

# INTRODUCTION

Wil Sebel, Gerrit Sebel, Dicky Sebel, Emmy IJzerman, Hermanus Bosch, Janny van Hoffen-Bosch, Winfried Bij, and Hans Muller. Others include Laurens Hooisma, who helped from Kampen; Martin Oordijk for locating descendants and relatives; Kevin Prenger for his historical advice. Jaap van Dort and Albert Bredenhoff helped realize the book. A major contribution in the publication of this book was Annemarie van Dijk, who guided and helped me. Her boundless enthusiasm helped me through this research and the documentation she prepared provided the starting point for it. Most of all I wish to thank my family, for listening to history stories.

While much has been written about the Second World War, there are still many untold stories. Tragedies and victories that are only remembered by a few people. It's been almost 75 years since the men died, however, finally they get the place they and their families deserve. Through the English publication of this book, it's possible for an international audience to gain insight into the suffering that resides in all war monuments. On behalf of the involved families, we are grateful that the history can be shared and that others will learn from it.

## Notes and justification

From the history of the execution on the Meppelerstraatweg on 31 March 1945 it can be derived that the traces of the Second World War are still present in our daily lives, such as through the monument that was placed there. History can be fickle and it's indeed true that there is an imbalance between the attention that all five men have received. The goal was to give them equal space, but there was simply more information available about some men than others. Family preference has beyond doubt played a role, although I tried to prevent this. The reader might notice that it didn't always work out that way.

About Willem Sebel and Jan Muller there was much more information available, partially due to their profession, which meant that more could also be written about them. About Wilhelmus van Dijk, Hermanus Bosch and Berend IJzerman I found out more through their descendants and written sources. Besides that, there were pictures of all the men and women involved.

The men and women of the Meppelerstraatweg I purposely called by their first names to increase readability of the book and to remain consistent. Still this was difficult, as Wilhelmus van Dijk and Willem Sebel were both called Willem in their daily lives. Furthermore, there was a brother called Piet van Dijk and a nephew with the same name, Piet van Dijk, which didn't help either, but I stuck to my choice.

For future research it could be useful to check the archive of Stichting 40-45, which provided compensation after the war and helped with the recovery of the Netherlands. There is information about Hermanus Bosch, but for the duration of the research these documents were inaccessible. Hermanus Bosch's contacts might also reveal more information about him. A possible source of information about Willem Sebel could be the interviews conducted by Bouwe van den Bergh with members of underground organisations. Hopefully this book can serve as a starting point for further research.

While conducting the interviews I heard many brave or exciting stories. Still I had to shift between what was likely to have happened, or what could have been touched by time or was twisted as they were passed down. Human memory is, after all, far from flawless. I stuck to a few principles. If someone had experienced something themselves or had seen it themselves, I assumed it was true. If it wasn't the case, but it was plausible because, for instance, it was verified by another source, or because it would have been a probable situation, I also incorporated it. Explanations that clarified situations I also used. A few rumours I incorporated as well, where I had to trust the interviewee. I clarified where this has happened.

A few aspects of history were difficult to track down and the evidence for some things was lacking. For instance, it could be that letters weren't sent to certain authorities or that files were incomplete. Other valuable sources were thrown away. Most difficult were sources where wrong information was given on purpose.

It was especially difficult to determine what happened exactly surrounding the Kamper Espionage Case where Berend IJzerman and Jan Muller were involved. I have tried to represent as accurately as possible what might have happened, as I think it did happen. The difficulty is that two of the three most prominent persons involved are dead and the last one gave conflicting explanations. He was promised drugs in exchange for his co-operation and during a later hearing he showed signs of insanity, mentioning conspiracies against him.

All sources were judged as to what degree they were likely to have happened. In a few cases I also point out where there are mistakes or if

# INTRODUCTION

things are unclear. At other moments more sources or more clarification in the sources would have been a great addition, but this was not always possible to find. Regardless, a large number of written sources have been brought together in order to cast a light on the lives of these men and women. These oral sources have been added to and therefore preserved for posterity.

Translation errors or historical mistakes that slipped into this work are mine for which I apologise. It's possible that another historian with the same sources will have a different reading of the material. Beyond doubt there are sources that have been missed or new sources to be uncovered. This book will certainly not be the last word about the execution on the Meppelerstraatweg, nor a definite claim as to what certainly happened. Rather it's what is most likely to have happened, but with the passing of time perhaps a new interpretation might arise in the future.

As a closing remark, I wish to thank you for reading this book. Without you the memory of the men and women of the Meppelerstraatweg wouldn't be kept alive. They died so that we could live in a free world, where people wouldn't be discriminated against or segregated. They acted in the belief that they were making a better world for everyone. They sacrificed themselves so that people could openly discuss, disagree and do what they want. Let's not forget that.

Peter van Dijk and Maria te Wierike, ca. 1940. (*Van Dijk family archive*)

# TRAGEDY AND BETRAYAL IN THE DUTCH RESISTANCE

Jan Goedings and Wilhelmina van Dijk at their marriage, ca. 1933. (*Van Dijk family archive*)

# Chapter 1

# A Horrid Execution

In the early morning of 31 March 1945, two German vehicles stopped at the Meppelerstraatweg in Zwolle; a car and a bus. From the bus came five men who were lined up at one side of the street between the trees, while opposite them stood ten members of the German *Ordnungspolizei*. The five men between the trees were: Wilhelmus Antonius Maria van Dijk, Johannes Albertus Muller, Berend Jan IJzerman, Hermanus Bosch and Willem Sebel.

The men had been captured in the previous weeks by the *Sicherheitsdienst* (SD) for various crimes: weapon possession, espionage or other offences. They were brought together by the occupying powers and would die together as part of a reprisal for a blown-up railway bridge.

On both sides of the Meppelerstraatweg people had come together, chance passers-by that would be unwanted witnesses to a cruel act. Some of them would spend the rest of their lives with a trauma from that fatal morning.

As soon as the order was given, a salvo followed that ended the lives of the Dutchmen. Swiftly afterwards *coup-de-grâce* shots followed to ensure that the five men were truly dead. Afterwards the firing squad departed and the bodies were left behind.

Why was this harsh example necessary? What would the five men have thought in their final moments? Why were they captured? What marks were left this morning on the lives of their women and children? It's not possible to answer all these questions. However, instead the lives of the men and their sacrifice are given a place in history. Thanks to the things they did, the current Dutch population can live in freedom.

To properly understand the men, they will be treated separately. What did they experience during the Second World War? What did they do to be condemned to death and what impact did this have on their families?

# TRAGEDY AND BETRAYAL IN THE DUTCH RESISTANCE

The archive material is leading this research, supplemented by various other sources. The most important literature consists of Kees Ribbens, *Bewogen Jaren: Zwolle in de Tweede Wereldoorlog;* Coen Hilbrink et al., *De Pruus komt: Overijssel in de Tweede Wereldoorlog*; Wolter Noordman, *De vijftien executies: Liquidaties aan de IJsseloever, April 1945;* Marten Roël, *Hotel van Gijtenbeek in de oorlog: Het verzetsleven van J. H. Roël.*[1] Finally there were conversations with descendants and witnesses to give a broader picture of the men's lives.

Willem Sebel, Hermanus Bosch and Wilhelmus van Dijk will be treated separately. Berend IJzerman and Johannes Muller will be examined together, because their lives were interwoven. Afterwards we will look at the period the men spent in the Zwolse *Huis van Bewaring,* a special type of prison where criminals were kept until they could be tried and sentenced. The families were left without information during that time and they will also be studied. At the end the traces of war will be reviewed.

Before the examining can start, it's important to explain a few terms. As Bert-Jan Hartman has noted in his research on local Resistance in Zwolle during the Second World War,[2] there's a difference between the Resistance, the illegal organisations and the underground. The Resistance can be actions that are anti-German and can be personal as well as a collective act. An example could be listening to prohibited radio stations or refusing to sign a statement confirming one's Aryan ancestors, an *Ariërverklaring.* Illegal activities concerned everything that was prohibited by the German law and regulations. Illegal work could, for instance, be helping Allied pilots or committing sabotage to German vehicles. Underground referred to the secret nature of the work, which was done without the Germans or their institutions being aware of what was going on. This is in contrast to public Resistance, such as a strike, where the Germans could see who was involved.

# Chapter 2

# The Five Men and Their Families

The five men who were lined up in the early morning between the trees of the Meppelerstraatweg, Zwolle, were a diverse company. The youngest was 31 years old, the oldest was 54. Amongst them was a Knight in the Order of Oranje-Nassau and a bailiff in hiding.* Two were born in Kampen and only one of them was born in Zwolle. One was captured after a weapon was discovered at his home. Two others were present because they confessed to espionage. One helped railway personnel in hiding with acquiring their wages. One was there, even though he had managed to hide a pistol successfully when the Germans were searching his home. All of them were fathers and had wives and children hoping for their swift return. Their backgrounds divided them, but they had fought back against the German occupiers. The fatal consequences of that brought them together between the trees of the Meppelerstraatweg.

Wilhelmus van Dijk, date unknown. (*Van Dijk family archive*)

---

\* Note on translation: In Dutch he was a *parketwachter*, which is something like a prison guard and a person that is present in court to make the suspect behave and escort him/her.

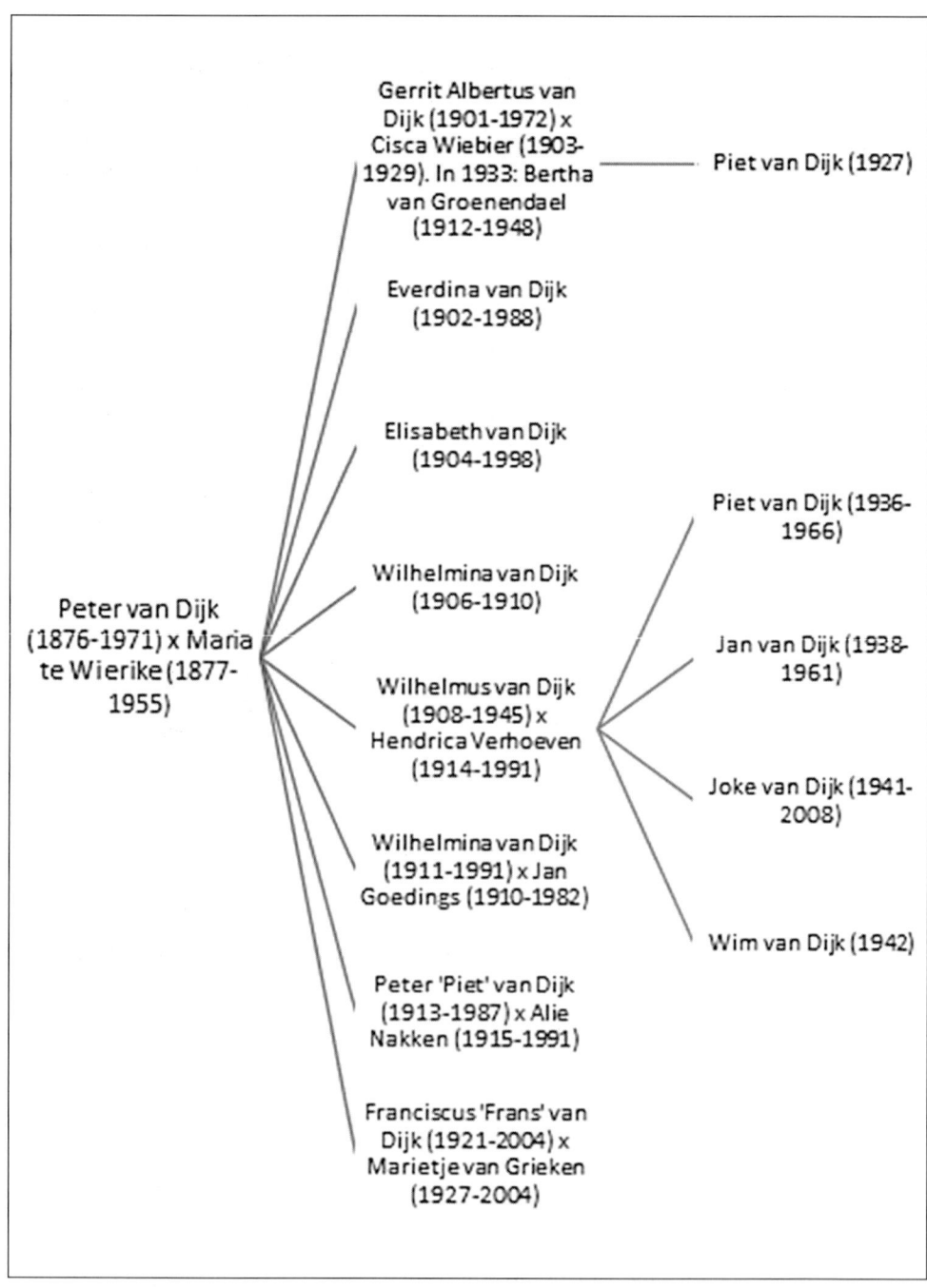

The children of Peter and Maria van Dijk, partially filled in with partners and grandchildren. (Van Dijk family archive)

# THE FIVE MEN AND THEIR FAMILIES

The marriage of Piet van Dijk, the brother, with Allie Nakken. On the far left is Wilhemus van Dijk, behind him Frans van Dijk. Far right is Gerrit van Dijk. In the middle at the front is Piet van Dijk, the son of Gerrit. Standing behind Piet are Peter and Maria van Dijk, the parents of the brothers, 1943. (*Van Dijk family archive*)

## Wilhelmus Antonius Maria van Dijk

*Truckdriver and other professions*

Wilhelmus van Dijk, or 'Willem', as he was known, was born on 10 November 1908 in Zwolle. He was the fifth child of Peter van Dijk (1876) and Maria te Wierike (1877). She was raised as a Catholic, while he wasn't, so he converted to Catholicism. The two married on 14 February 1901 and had nine children, of whom eight survived. During his baptism, Wilhelmus was given the Catholic name Maria. Like his father, Wilhelmus started working as a warehouseman.[1]

On 20 November 1931, Wilhelmus left to go to Uden in Noord-Brabant, a Dutch province to the south of Overijssel. Here he started working at a farm and helped with transporting the cattle. It was there that he met one of the farmer's daughters, Hendrica Verhoeven, who was born on 2 April 1914. She had spent some time in Zwolle and returned in 1933. Due to the large family, she and a sister were sent to Zwolle to do domestic work in a hospital. Because they had lived in the same city, Wilhelmus and Hendrica will have spent many nights talking about Zwolle. When Wilhelmus moved back to Zwolle two years later Hendrica went after him. They married on 5 December 1935 and had four children, Piet, Jan, Joke and Wim. At first they lived on the Van Rossumstraat 22, but later they moved to the Balistraat 24.[2]

Wilhelmus had a close relationship with his brothers Gerrit and Peter, nicknamed 'Piet', born respectively in 1901 and 1913. They attempted many things together, although the youngest brother, Frans, born in 1921, was usually left out. For a while Gerrit and Wilhelmus had their own transport company, where Gerrit took care of the administration and Wilhelmus drove the heavy loads. They didn't have the company for long, as business wasn't going well. Later they had a fish shop, where their father worked frying the shrimps. Sadly this venture also failed. The Great Depression wasn't kind to the two brothers. Eventually Wilhelmus started as a mechanic at a garage and had his own motorcycle.[3]

Although the family was raised as Catholics, the brothers weren't zealous in their faith. Gerrit and Wilhelmus were often already in the pub before the mass had ended. In his spare time, Wilhelmus collected the adventures of Tarzan that appeared in the newspapers which he cut out and put in a book.

## *'Rather on the rubble than underneath'*

During the Second World War Wilhelmus worked in Germany for a period. Poverty and German propaganda had seduced him into German service. While in Germany he worked as a driver in Bad-Driburg and Paderborn, while Hendrica was left in Zwolle with the children. During the Allied bombardments on German cities, Wilhelmus refused to go into the shelters, because as he said himself: *'Rather on the rubble than underneath'*.[4]

During Wilhelmus's voluntary stay in Germany, his brother Gerrit was involved with changing the Zwolle department of the *Nederlandse Unie* to a Resistance organization. The *Nederlandse Unie* was a political movement raised in 1940 as a counterpart to the pro-German *Nationaal-Socialistische Beweging* (NSB).[5]

Money seems to have been his biggest drive, as is related in a letter from Gerrit to Wilhelmus, dated 30 July 1941:

> 'Dear brother Wilhelm, your writing read and re-read with interest, for that thank you. Regarding the health status of

our extended family … all's well. You write that there is more money to earn than in Holland and ask me to come to Germany? Yes brother… that could be, but since I have a regular job… that won't do. Indeed, we would benefit a lot from each other, we know each other too well for that. I would like to take a look, especially the natural beauty fascinates me again and again. Capturing such natural scenes on canvas, that would indeed be my wish. Well, brother, hotcakes simply aren't baked, we must take life as she is and we accept her in all her capriciousness. So far to answers your questions. Now to the point of live [*ing*] in Zwolle. Since your departure from Zwolle life has gotten more expensive and we can't get enough [*food*] anymore. e.g. potatoes, vegetables (still expensive) baked fish, we don't know anymore. Fat is impossible to get. One ounce of meat with bone per person per week, no beer etc. etc. You see brother … softly we are scraping by. Shoemakers are busy with cutting holes in our belts. The belt is getting tighter and tighter. Well… we live and that's most important. After rain comes sunshine! Now brother, greetings from all and especially your brother Gerrrit. See you in 14 days.'[6]

It is unknown how or why Wilhelmus came back from Germany. On 15 May 1942 he was still working there. Possibly he managed to get a job in Zwolle or could he have returned because the underground organisations were doing well, so that it wasn't necessary to work in Germany to get foodstuffs. A decisive factor could be that Hendrica was pregnant and Wilhelmus was allowed to return home for the birth of his son.[7]

On his return from Germany in May 1943, Wilhelmus joined the illegal organization of Henk Beernink, who was known as 'De Groene', *The Green*. This group was special as it was dedicated to various aspects of the underground activities, instead of just one. People in hiding were helped, documents were forged and sabotage committed.[8]

Brothers Gerrit and Piet were also part of this organization. Gerrit operated under the aliases Albertus van Dam, Albertus van der Wal, and Willemsen and took up a leading position in the group. He had left-leaning political views and was involved in the Resistance from 1941. He did various things, such as setting up a message service.[9]

Wilhelmus van Dijk, middle, with Gerrit van Dijk, right, on a terrace, ca. 1940-1944. (*Van Dijk family archive*)

Brother Piet was involved with transporting weapons. Once he walked through Zwolle with a handcar full of weapons, hidden only under a sail.

The youngest brother Frans remained an outsider and volunteered for the *Reichsarbeitsdienst,* the German Labour service. In Schalkhaar there was a police training centre, where there was a strong national socialistic influence. Here Frans tried to apply but was rejected. Later his older brothers had a talk with him to prevent him from hanging out too much with Germans. 'If you do that, then I'll shoot you next time I see you.' Frans became so frightened by this, that he never spoke with the Germans again.

An important event that could have influenced the family Van Dijk to actively join 'De Groene' and his organization, could be the deportation of the Jewish family Zilverberg. They lived at the Holtenbroekerweg 1, in the same street as several members of the family Van Dijk. When the family was picked up, the girls were crying for their mother. On 21 May 1943 they died with their parents in extermination camp Sobibor.[10]

Due to the diverse nature of the illegal organisation 'De Groene', Wilhelmus was also involved in several things. Weapons were kept at his house and messages passed on. Besides that, uniforms and a radio were hidden at his house. Hendrica also transported weapons in the

## THE FIVE MEN AND THEIR FAMILIES

The deported Jetje and Esther (Elly) Zilverberg, living on the Holtenbroekerweg 1. On 21 May 1943 they were deported with their parents Mozes and Reintje Zilverberg and murdered in Sobibor. (*Historisch Centrum Overijssel*)

carriers of her bike and once she warned Gerrit at his secret address that a dangerous situation was about to arise.[11]

Wilhelmus also took care of others. A little brother and sister of Hendrica stayed at the Balistraat 23. Arnoldus, Hendrica's younger brother, came along with the move in August 1940 and left on 18 March 1941. Theodora, the younger sister, stayed from 3 June 1942 to 11 September 1943. During the *hongerwinter* (Hunger Winter) of 1944-1945, Hendrica's sister from Amsterdam stayed at her house.[12]

For a period, a deserter from the German army was hidden at Wilhelmus's house. Besides that, Wilhelmus provided food for his neighbour, the family Sattler who lived on the Balistraat 22. Butter, potatoes, flour and meat were collected by motorcycle in Staphorst, where he got the food from farmers or bought it.[13]

Through the backyard the food was handed to the family Sattler. Sometimes they paid cash, other times they traded cigarettes, or it was given away for free. Aeldert Sattler, the father of the family, was a police officer and supplied the illegal organizations in Zwolle with information. Due to this, he regularly changed address. The family Sattler also had a son, Hendrik, who was shot on 17 February 1945 during a reprisal.[14]

## TRAGEDY AND BETRAYAL IN THE DUTCH RESISTANCE

Around New Year 1945 two members of the American Air Force stayed at Wilhelmus's house. Later they would be sent to the south of the Netherlands. One day Piet, the son of Gerrit van Dijk, walked in and heard only English. While he couldn't understand it, he was quick to realize that the two men in civilian clothes were allied air personnel and not just regular visitors. Since Wilhelmus and Hendrica were incapable of speaking English, they must have had outside help with translation.[15]

It is certain that at least two pilots were hidden for some time at the Balistraat 24. One pilot's name could not be recalled, but the other one was co-pilot Richard 'Dick' Fuller, from Hollywood, California. He was a member of the 708th squadron of the 447th Bomber Group from the American forces in England.

On 6 December 1944, the bomber *Blanco Diablo* (B-17G 42-102658) was hit by Flak, German anti-aircraft guns, above Mersburg. The crew was forced to bail about above Staphorst. All, except Joe

The aircrew of the *Blanco Diablo*, standing (L to R): Joe Marlowe, Loel Bishop, Don Holmes, Hank Rutkowski, Lowell Strain, Harold Derr. Sitting: Howard Demaillie, Chuck Olson, Bill Leader, Dick Fuller, 1944. (*American Air Museum*)

## THE FIVE MEN AND THEIR FAMILIES

Marlowe, whose parachute refused to open, managed to reach the ground safely. Eventually all crew members were captured, except for Dick Fuller, who managed to evade capture. He was picked up by Arend Boers in the neighbourhood of Staphorst, who fed him. Afterwards his journey went towards Meppel, then back to Staphorst, before going to Zwolle. 'Auntie Nel', *Tante Nel,* an alias of a lady Meyer-Noach from the Molenweg 289 in Zwolle brought Fuller to Wilhelmus's home. He stayed there for three days before he went on to Albertus Huiberts, living on the Hertenstraat 38 in Zwolle. He was escorted to that address by two unknown men.[16]

There is at least one action where Wilhelmus was almost certainly involved, which is the sabotage of German trucks. In the book *Bewogen Jaren* by Kees Ribbens, there is the following passage:

> Begin September 1944 '*De Groene*' launched a number of activities in the context of the Allied advance. On the night of 3 to 4 September 1944, two men with a gun forced a driver at the Schutte garage to hand over a key of the building. The ignition from two trucks was removed and the crankcases filled with sand. Later the same happened at another garage owner. That same night six men entered a farmyard. While two guards were facing the wall, a threshing machine was disabled. The next night again two trucks were sabotaged in a garage. Also on September 5th and September 7th '*De Groene*' struck and disabled two German trucks. These actions were undertaken to hinder the transport of the Germans as much as possible.[17]

It is likely that Wilhelmus was involved in this operation. While it's impossible to determine it for certain, there are several remarkable circumstances. First Wilhelmus worked at a garage and had as a mechanic the necessary experience with trucks and operating them. Besides that, he had a *Wehrmacht*-toolset for cars at his home during his arrest. It could be that he used this for the disabling actions or that he took the set during the actions. In the application for the Resistance Memorial Cross, the *Verzetsherdenkingskruis,* a medal that was awarded in the 1980s to members of the Dutch Resistance, a reference was made to sabotage that Wilhelmus had committed. Jan de Graver, who was a member of the illegal organization and was credited as a source, had confirmed the sabotage. Brother Gerrit also referred to sabotage and breaking into *Wehrmacht* units in his service record. While it's impossible to claim for certain that Wilhelmus was really involved in these actions against German trucks, there are several remarkable circumstances that hint towards it.[18]

## The weapon in the cupboard

The situation changed for the Zwolse illegal organisations when Henk Beernink, the leader of 'De Groene', was shot on 8 February 1945 and his notebook was found by the German *Sicherheitsdienst* (SD). Due to this information, they could make various arrests. As a precaution the uniforms, a stencil machine, and almost all the weapons and ammunition were brought from Wilhelmus's house to Piet's address. Only one small calibre pistol was kept and Hendrica hid it in the kitchen cupboard behind a stack of plates. It was assumed to be safe there.

On the morning of 18 March 1945, the SD was carrying out several arrests. Previously they went to the old house of Gerrit, on the Holtenbroekerweg 12, but the family was already hidden elsewhere. After the SD had destroyed the furniture, they moved on.

At the same time, a warning was sent to Wilhelmus that he was possibly in danger and should go into hiding. However, Wilhelmus didn't heed this advice as he believed the Germans couldn't prove anything against him and he doubted they would find anything during a house search. Instead he helped to repair the bike of an acquaintance, Thijs Brouwer, as he had promised.[19]

Around 12 o'clock members of the SD rang the doorbell. A team was gathered outside, under the command of the Dutchman Piet Richard Cieraard, who was dressed in civilian clothing. He was a fanatical member of the SD. Born in 1921, in 1944 he became a member of the SD in Zwolle, after he spent some time as a bodyguard to NSB-leader Anton Mussert. After he arrived in Zwolle he swiftly became notorious because he acted openly during the tracking down and arresting members of the Resistance and the illegal organisations.[20]

Wilhelmus wanted to escape through the back of the house, but this was impossible, because one of the children had opened the door. The

## THE FIVE MEN AND THEIR FAMILIES

occupants of the house were searched for weapons and put under guard in the living room, while the rest of the SD-members searched the home. This was done with a heavy-handed approach, as the floor was broken open and the radio was discovered. Foodstuffs were confiscated and the pistol in the cupboard was also found by the SD. Hendrica was ordered to take the children to another address in the neighbourhood and return immediately.

At the same time a car was driven in front of the house and four people ordered to get in: Wilhelmus, Hendrica, Hendrica's sister and Thijs Brouwer. At the same time Mrs Sattler and her children were looking through their window and Hendrica waved to them as they departed. The four adults were brought by car to the *Dienststelle* (Department) of the SD at the Van Nahuysplein.[21]

Besides the pistol, other things were confiscated, including a roll of carpet, a *Wehrmacht*-binocular, a *Wehrmacht*-vehicle toolset as well as meat from an illegally butchered pig and five kilos of butter.[22] Due to the confiscated items and the four arrested people, two members of the SD had to stay in the house to wait until they could be picked up. Cieraad had told them which possessions they needed to confiscate.[23]

It wouldn't have mattered if Wilhelmus had kept the pistol or not, because the SD had arrived with orders to arrest him. During interrogations and from Henk Beernink's notebook, they had enough information to know that Gerrit van Dijk and Wilhelmus van Dijk were family. Besides that, the SD knew that Wilhelmus was involved in illegal activities and that there were potentially weapons in the house. This was confirmed when they discovered the radio under the floor, the pistol in the kitchen cupboard, the *Wehrmacht*-equipment and the foodstuffs.[24]

It is interesting to note that the pistol wasn't mentioned in the list of confiscated goods, while Hendrica did mention it in her testimony. A possible explanation could be that someone forgot to write it down. Another possibility could be that this pistol was pilfered by a member of the SD. Pilfering often occurred and weapon possession was mentioned in the list of items that was handed to the officer responsible for the execution.[25]

However, another explanation, that should be used with care, is derived from Cieraad, the man in charge of the arrest. After his arrest he lied a great deal and this could be one of his lies. He spoke about a messenger *Zuster Jo,* 'Sister Jo', who was also known as Neijboom, who told the Germans...

> 'entirely voluntarily and with a certain cynicism, very calm and while smoking uncountable cigarettes' among other information that: 'Van Dijk, Balistraat 24, is in possession of a radio set and furthermore an English soldier and an Austrian [*are*] in hiding in his home.' *This note was in accordance with [...] a note found in the diary of a prominent illegal worker*: 'v. Dijk, Balistraat 24: 1 pilot.'

Cieraad explained this after the war and according to him the messenger Neijboom had the feeling that she had been abandoned and therefore told this. To what degree this is the truth, is unknown.[26]

Wilhelmus van Dijk and the three others weren't the only ones that were arrested that day. After the four adults were taken away, Gerhardus LeLoux, the owner of the garage where Wilhelmus worked and his neighbour across the street, went over to the house for more information. He had seen how his mechanic had been taken away and wanted to know what had happened. After he rang the doorbell, a German in uniform opened the door and told LeLoux to come in and wait until his chief returned to decide what to do.

After approximately half an hour Cieraad returned, still dressed in civilian clothes. When he was informed that LeLoux was Wilhelmus's boss, he immediately said: 'That guy also comes with us.' LeLoux had to sit in the car and was brought to the *Dienststelle* of the SD. There his papers were checked by SD-member Walter Bartels, Cieraad's superior, and send home again. LeLoux told of this event: 'I was very surprised by the performance of this Dutchman [Cieraad], as he arrested me as a Dutchman, while I was released immediately by a German.'[27]

## Hermanus Bosch

*Working at a printing house*

Hermanus Bosch was born on 5 January 1914 in Kampen, the son of a warehouseman who later became a coal trader. His father was

## THE FIVE MEN AND THEIR FAMILIES

Hermannus Bosch and his mother was Hilligje Selles. The family lived at the Vloeddijk 37 in Kampen and was of the Dutch Reformed faith. After passing his primary education, Hermanus studied at a high school for three years.

On 30 August 1929, Hermanus went to Amsterdam, but returned on 6 November 1931 to Kampen. He left Kampen again on 1 May 1933 to go to Leeuwarden, where he worked as a volunteer in a printing house for some time, then he left for Groningen on 9 October 1935. He lived at the Wassenberghstraat 66b, while he worked as a volunteer at a press again.[28]

On 18 June 1934 Hermanus was called up for conscription, as his number, 24, had come up. He was drafted into the 1st Infantry Regiment, destined for non-commissioned officer training due to his former education. His base was Assen but he did not stay long as on 25 June Hermanus went to the specialist company of the 19th Infantry Regiment in Arnhem. There he followed a course to be a telephone operator and signalman. He passed his training and received a note as an 'extraordinary trained signaller and telephone operator'. Besides that, he was a good shot and grenade thrower.

Hermanus Bosch, date unknown. (*NIOD*)

On 3 September Hermanus went to the advance guard detachment of the 19th Infantry Regiment stationed in Doesburg. On 22 September he returned to the specialist company of the 19th Infantry Regiment. On 29 September he was promoted to corporal and to titular-sergeant on 2 February 1935. Shortly afterwards he became ill and needed to be taken to hospital on 18 February, before he was released again on 27 February. He returned to the specialist company of the 1st Infantry Regiment in Assen. On 17 March 1935, a day before he could take his long-term leave, he was promoted to sergeant.[29]

On 22 August 1936 Hermanus moved to Amsterdam, to the Johan Verhulststraat 28, where later he would move within the same street, and then twice within the same city. On 19 November 1941 he left for Kampen and moved in on the Cellesweg 13. Precisely a year later he moved to Zwolle.[30]

# TRAGEDY AND BETRAYAL IN THE DUTCH RESISTANCE

On 29 August 1939, Hermanus was back in arms, in the service of the 3rd Battalion of the 25th Infantry Regiment, where he was added to the staff. On 25 August the regiment had started with the advance mobilization. Hermanus himself arrived only on 29 August on the first day of the mobilization. The arrival of the personnel went well, the detachments were brought up to full strength and equipment was supplemented. Horses and vehicles were provided and improvised kitchen wagons established. The second day everything that wasn't finished the day before was taken care of.[31]

On 1 September the staff of the battalion was encamped in the Roman Catholic boys' school in Jutphaas. On 25 September, the later commander of the Dutch Army, Henri Winkelman, visited the battalion and combat positions were taken up. On 2 November there was another important visitor, Prince Bernhard of Lippe Biesterfeld.

The threat of war was tangible. On 9 November security was heightened out of fear of potential spies in Dutch uniforms and the bridges were guarded to prevent any landings. A day later leave was cancelled.[32]

On 18 April 1940, the battalion left Jutphaas at 6am and went to Beesd where the staff was housed in the village. From 27 April onwards periodic leave was allowed for a few men but on 7 May this was cancelled again, except for the men involved in the army industries. The guards were doubled.

On 9 May the battalion received the order at 10pm that the next day, 10 May all positions must be fully manned. From 4am German planes were spotted and where possible the positions were improved and strengthened. By radio it was announced that the Dutch government rejected the German ultimatum and that the Netherlands were at war with Germany. The Allies were England, France and Belgium.

On 11 May the battalion received an order to detach a company to the bridge in Vianen to guard the crossing of the River Lek. The 2nd company was chosen for this task. Later another order came to direct a company to Zijderveld and for this task the 1st company was chosen.

On 12 May at 9am the order was received to move to Herwijnen where the northern shore of the Waal was to be occupied. The next day, at 8am, the order was given to return to Beesd, whereupon the

## THE FIVE MEN AND THEIR FAMILIES

men were loaded into cars at 2pm. From here they were brought to Vianen and at 5.30pm the battalion received the order to march to the Kromhoutkazerne. Afterwards the men were ordered to march in the direction of Jutphaas and wait until they were relieved by the 10th Infantry Regiment.[33]

At 3.30am a machinegun company took up positions in front of the unit, flanked by two sections of soldiers from the third company slightly behind them. The battalion was ready for combat. However, it didn't come to violence, because by 6.30pm the battalion stood ready to march towards the fortresses of Vossegat and Lunetten to occupy them. Later they received the message from General Winkelman that the fighting ceased. The Germans had bombed Rotterdam, inflicting heavy casualties, and threatened to do the same to Utrecht. To spare civilian casualties, Winkelman capitulated.

The battalion stayed in Jutphaas and on 20 May had to move to Houten within four hours, in order to clear space for the 10th Infantry Regiment. On 24 May the regiment to which the battalion belonged was united again and a day later every man from the battalion had reported again. Half of the men were sent on long-term leave. Hermanus stayed with the army until 14 July 1940. A day later the Dutch army ceased to exist on the orders of the Germans.[34]

For Hermanus the Battle of the Netherlands consisted of a lot of marching to different locations and no combat. However, the training that he had while in the army, he would put to use later. Instead of being used in a conventional war, he would use them in the underground struggle.

## *A marriage during times of war*

In Zwolle Hermanus had met Gerharda Peters, who worked as a saleswoman in C&A. She was born on 29 August 1918, the daughter of a newspaper compositor. They married on 20 November 1942. Shortly before the ceremony the couple was picked up at the house of Gerharda's parents at the Assendorperstraat 167A in Zwolle and left for the city hall where the necessary documents had to be signed. From there the couple went by carriage to the reformed church, where the marriage was sealed and by carriage the couple returned for the party.

# TRAGEDY AND BETRAYAL IN THE DUTCH RESISTANCE

Hermanus Bosch and Gerharda Peters, date unknown. (*Bosch family archive*)

Hermanus Bosch and Gerharda Peters on their wedding day, 20 November 1942. (*Bosch family archive*)

# THE FIVE MEN AND THEIR FAMILIES

During the festivities, a song was sung written specially for the event. It used the melody of another song, *'Heidewietska vooruit geef gas'* (Heidewietska, forward accelerate) by Willy Derby, but with changed lyrics.

*Nu Bosch en Peters saam zijn vereend,*
*Klinke ons lied hartelijk gemeend,*
*En voorlopig aan de Bitterweg,*
*Hebben ze geen pech,*
*Nu met hun twee blij en tevree,*
*Varen ze saam op d'huwelijkszee,*
*Samen de lusten, maar ook samen de last*
*Dan gaat het goed, dat weet ik vast.*

*Refrein:*
*Hoog het feestlied, het glas er bij,*
*Voor Bruidegom en Bruidje allebei,*
*Wij wensen hun nog mening jaartje,*
*Heel vaak bezoek van 't Ooievaartje,*
*Hoog het feestlied, het glas er bij,*
*Voor Bruidegrom en Bruidje allebei.*

*Als Herman thuis komt is hij blij en tevree*
*Dan krijgt hij steeds koekjes bij de thee,*
*Voor echt geluk behoeft men geen millioen*
*Maar alleen een zoen,*
*Zingt dus ons lied vrolijk en luid,*
*Samen ter eer van Bruidegom en Bruid,*
*Vrolijk ons allen bij elkander geschaard,*
*Herman en Gerrie zijn het waard.*

*Hoog het feestlied, het glas er bij,*
*Voor Bruidegom en Bruidje allebei,*
*Wij wensen hun nog mening jaartje,*
*Heel vaak bezoek van 't Ooievaartje,*
*Hoog het feestlied, het glas er bij,*
*Voor Bruidegom en Bruidje allebei.*

Loosely translated:
Now Bosch and Peters have been united
Sound our song truly meant
And for now at the Bitterweg
Have they got no bad luck
Now they're together happy and well
Sailing together on the marriage sea
Together the loves and the burden
Then it will be all right, I'm certain

Sing the song, raise the glass
For the groom and bride
We wish them many years
And often a visit from the stork
Sing the song, raise the glass
For the groom and bride

When Herman comes home, he's happy and well.
He'll always get cookies with thee.
For true happiness you don't need a million
Only a kiss.
So sing our song happy and loud
Together for the groom and bride.
Happy together we came
For Herman and Gerrie are worth it.

Sing the song, raise the glass
For the groom and bride
We wish them many years
And often a visit from the stork
Sing the song, raise the glass
For the groom and bride

The couple moved in to the Bitterstraat 69a and had their first child in November 1943, who was given the same name as his father: Herman.

## *Moving to the Korenbloemstraat*

During the Second World War Herman became involved with the illegal organisations in Friesland and Groningen but stayed in Zwolle. Often Hermanus was in contact with Henk Beernink from the underground organisation 'De Groene'. Hermanus's aliases were Hans Berkhout and Dik Bosch. One of the reasons he chose Hans Berkhout was so that his initials H.B. would be the same. At his home Hermanus hid weapons.[35]

After the successful raid on the *Huis van Bewaring* (House of Detention) in Leeuwarden on 8 December 1944, a so-called 'Piet Kramer' was hidden at the Hermanus home. The true name of this person was Piet Oberman and he led the action against the prison and managed to liberate fifty-one people. Oberman's pistol was hidden in the diapers of little Herman.[36]

Besides Piet Oberman, Hermanus was also in contact with Piet van den Berg and Johannes van Bijnen. Van Bijnen was the national sabotage commander until he was killed. He commanded approximately forty-five fighting groups, called *Knokploegen* throughout the Netherlands. He was fatally wounded during a firefight with a German patrol on 22 November 1944, when he was in Apeldoorn to see if it was possible to liberate prisoners from the local barracks. Hermanus's house was described as the 'centre and refuge of the KP-leadership in the North'.[37]

Meetings were held with Hermanus and others at a friendly address at the Vispoortenplas 3, where there was an optician at the ground floor. The family that lived there was also named Bosch and could have been potentially family through Jan Bosch (1785-1862) who came from Ommen. The rear entrance of the house was perpendicular to the front entrance, which made it possible to enter the house unseen. On Sunday, when the family in residence was in church, Hermanus and other people came in through the rear door to meet unseen.[38]

Hermanus came by this address when Sara Bosch-Bramer, who was married to Machiel Bosch, the owner of the house, went on a maternity visit and in the talk that followed it became obvious that Machiel and

## THE FIVE MEN AND THEIR FAMILIES

Sara Bosch too wished to do something against the German occupiers. Shortly afterwards the question came whether Hermanus and others could meet at that address.[39] If people came for Hermanus Bosch, then they would go to the optician and ask if Hans Berkhout was present. As a code they said: 'I come from Kampen,' thereupon the children of the Vispoortenplas 3 went to get Hermanus Bosch, who lived nearby.[40]

Once Sara Bosch-Bramer and her eldest daughter received a bonbon from Hermanus Bosch. At that time it was an extraordinary gift and hard to come by. The family also managed to get electricity, which was fixed with the help of a brother of the late professor Jan Willem Schulte Nordholt. That the family had electricity brought about remarkable situations, as the store servants were not supposed to know that it was present. The lenses of the glasses were ground at an NSB-optician, Heukels.[41]

A friendly typist, and also messenger, was often upstairs working at the Vispoortenplas 3. Sometimes she joined the family for dinner, but at others she was gone for a long time. On orange paper she worked out the pieces that she had been given. The typing machine was hidden in a closet under Sara Bosch-Brame's dresses.[42]

Two unverified rumours state that Hermanus Bosch was once seen by his parents-in-law wearing a German uniform. It must have been a shock for them to see their son-in-law wearing the oppressor's uniform. The other rumour was that that he once transported weapons in the pram.[43]

At the end of January 1945 the family swapped houses with another family and moved to the Korenbloemstraat 16. The reason was that Hermanus didn't feel comfortable in his old house when there was a detachment of *Organisation Todt* (OT) opposite him. *Organisation Todt* supplied labourers to the occupying forces and included people that worked for the Germans on defensive lines on the shores of the IJssel. During the moving, the weapons were brought to another address.[44]

### *The hidden pistol*

Hermanus felt uncomfortable without a gun and asked for a new one. This was delivered on the evening of 17 March 1945 and hidden in the attic. The next day at 8am the doorbell rang. The family was still in bed, but the *Sicherheitsdienst* was already up. Hermanus considered an escape through the back of the house, but there were also uniformed men there.[45] After getting dressed, he opened the door for the Germans.

# TRAGEDY AND BETRAYAL IN THE DUTCH RESISTANCE

Willy Mönnich, 1946. (*National Archives*)

Four members of the SD, which included Willy Mönnich and Reinhard Stuck, entered the house and started searching. Two SD-members went directly to the attic and Hermanus went after them. Despite the searching, Hermanus managed to get the pistol unseen and once downstairs again he slipped this to Gerharda, while the SD was still looking around the house. She hid it under her clothes so that the SD wouldn't find it.[46]

Because the SD couldn't find anything, they switched tactics. They asked Hermanus if he knew Henk Beernink or 'De Groene'. Hermanus denied this and the same questions were asked of Gerharda, who also gave negative answers. During this interrogation a German car came out of an alley and stopped in front of the house. Despite the denials, Hermanus was ordered to get in and brought to the Zwolse *Huis van Bewaring* where he was locked up.[47]

How Hermanus managed to get the pistol, without discovery by the two SD-members that were still searching the attic, and then hand it to Gerharda is unknown. Neither does it become clear why Hermanus was arrested. Considering how the SD operated, there could have been an (un)intentional traitor involved, but it doesn't necessarily become clear from the sources. Notorious SD-member Cieraard stated, in a potentially lying confession, that information had been given by Herman Meijer, who operated under the alias of Red Tonny, *Rode Tonny*. What information this was or how Meijer was in contact with Bosch, is unclear. Most curious is the arrival of the pistol and the timing of the house search.[48]

It is remarkable that during the arrest of Hermanus there had been no evidence acquired. The sources are silent about the nature of the information that had been given about him. Despite all this, Hermanus was still arrested.

## THE FIVE MEN AND THEIR FAMILIES

The notes left by Gerrit van Dijk suggest that he and Hermanus had been in contact with each other. Possibly they met through the *Nederlandse Unie*, the political party. Gerrit was active in the region of Zwolle and Hermanus could have helped with the printing considering his background.

In the book *Het Grote Gebod* the house of Hermanus Bosch is described as a contact address for the *Landelijke KnokPloegen* (National Fight Groups), while documents for the L.O., *Landelijke Organisatie voor Hulp aan Onderduikers* (National Organisation for Help to People in Hiding) and the LKP show that Piet Oberman and Piet van den Berg, who were part of the top of the LKP, often visited his place.[49] Piet Oberman was part of the *Knokploeg Friesland* and under the orders of the *Binnenlandse Strijdkrachten* (Interior Combat Forces) had raided the *Blokhuis*, the *Huis van Bewaring* in Leeuwarden on 8 December 1944. Because Gerharda also mentioned that her husband was active in illegal organisations in Friesland, it's assumed that both men were often at Hermanus's house.

## Willem Sebel

*With the Corps Police Force*

Willem Sebel was born on 4 April 1901 in Vlaardingen, the son of Gerrit Sebel and Maria van Dorp. His father was a fisherman. Willem was raised in the reformed church and had two sisters. His father died in January 1915. After finishing his primary education, Willem started working in a factory.[50]

On 4 April 1921 Willem Sebel was drafted for the Hussars. While first serving with the 3rd Regiment Hussars, he was transferred to the 2nd Regiment on 15 May 1922. A few months later, on 30 September 1922, his exercises were finished and he could take long-term leave.[51] After being out of service for two years, he returned to the 2nd Regiment on 16 June 1924. A day later he went over to the corps police force, where he joined the 3rd company in Nieuwersluis. The police forces were a new branch of service that was established in 1919 to function as the police service of the army.[52]

On 19 August 1924 Willem joined the Group Simpelveld and was allocated to the 4th company in Maastricht. A little more than two months

Willem Sebel with the 3rd Regiment Hussars, 1922. (*Sebel family archive*)

later on 20 October Willem joined the mounted department of the police force in Amsterdam, where he was allocated to the 2nd company. Due to his time with the Hussars he had probably developed an affinity with horses.[53]

On 16 January 1925 Willem signed up for five years with the police force. Two years had to be spent in active services, while the last three could be as a reserve. He didn't stay long, as on 3 April he went over to the mounted *Marechaussee* (Military Police), leaving the police force and signed up for six years of service and was allocated to the 3rd division of the Royal Netherlands *Marechaussee*.[54]

On 19 December 1928 he was granted the badge for six years of loyal service. On 3 April 1931 Willem volunteered for the Royal Dutch Army, destined for the Royal Netherlands *Marechaussee*. However, two years later he had to dismount and became a *marechaussee* on foot. He was stationed in Hardenberg, where he participated in social events. Unmarried men of the *marechaussee* were invited to eat with the widow Pot-Naarding. When there were celebrations for her thirty years of her cooking for the men, Willem was one of those that helped organise it. On 19 December 1934 he was awarded the bronze medal for twelve years of loyal service after which he requested to be released from the army which was granted on 31 December 1934.[55]

On 9 November 1934 the mayor of Hardenberg city, Christiaan F. Bramer received a letter in response to a message that had been sent out a day before. The position of patrolman had become vacant and Willem wished to show his interest.[56]

Willem did not drink a lot, was fond of shooting, was an anti-revolutionary and knew first aid. During shooting competitions, he received good marks. One of his reasons to apply was because he wished to marry Willemien Mensink and that wasn't possible with the police force and his chances of promotion were also marginal. Out of the eighty applicants, Willem was eventually chosen and shortly afterwards he married Wilhelmina 'Willemien' Mensink. This is where Wilhemus van Dijk and Willem Sebel's lives crossed, as they appeared on the same date in the same paper with their notice of marriage. Willem Sebel and Willemien Mensink had five children: four daughters and a son.[57]

Besides keeping order, Willem also carried out other functions in Hardenberg. On Queensday, at that time on 31 August, it was his task to hang out the flag at the official residence of Mayor Bramer.[58]

Willem was back in arms again when troubles started stirring at the Dutch-German border. He was in service in Hardenberg when the unrest within Europe became noticeable and was stationed in Hardenberg, where there were two command posts. During a potential German invasion, the soldiers in Hardenberg needed to delay the enemy as much as possible. They could do this by blowing up railway bridges, disabling the sluices or committing other acts of destruction.[59]

# TRAGEDY AND BETRAYAL IN THE DUTCH RESISTANCE

*Left*: Willem Sebel, ca. 1944. (*Sebel family archive*)

*Below*: Willem Sebel in uniform, 1932. (*Sebel family archive*)

# THE FIVE MEN AND THEIR FAMILIES

## *'A grim patriot'*

On 10 May 1940 the Netherlands were attacked. As soon as there was a message that German troops had crossed the borders, the bridges across the Overijsselskanaal were blown up. Afterwards Willem was ordered to destroyed the telephones at a command post. Firefights broke out with the advancing German troops and the Vechtbridge was about to be blown up. Willem managed to warn the residents of the neighbouring houses just in time. However, as a result of this, he became trapped between the retreating Dutch troops and the attacking German soldiers. With pride he spoke of the Dutch army: 'Tough guys, brave men; truly boys with courage. The Netherlands didn't fight in vain and Germany bought Holland dearly.'[60]

Early in the occupation Willem came in contact with the underground organisations. He was a loyal patriot who wished to fight against the German oppressor. Another illegal worker, A. Sportel from Hardenberg, wrote of him: 'Sebel was known as a grim patriot, who couldn't bear the great injustice that the Germans caused us. As a policeman he was sometimes dangerous for himself, as he spared nothing. This has sometimes been explained to him and he had a transfer as a result.'[61]

The punishment came on 15 April 1942 when Willem was stationed to the village Lutten. A possible explanation could be that Willem was spotted with an orange pin under his lapels. Someone noticed this and the new mayor gave him a penalty transfer within the municipality. Mayor Bramer had been fired a week before his retirement in November 1940, because he refused to dismiss his Jewish councillor and deputy mayor, Rudolf de Bruin. To what degree this story is true, is unknown, as the acting mayor that followed Bramer, Johannes van Oorschot, was given non-active status on 10 November 1942 by the *Der Reichskommissar für die besetzten Niederländischen Gebiete*, Arthur Seyss-Inquart, and relieved of his function in 1943. The NSB-mayor that followed him, Frederik Overbeek, only came in 1943, after Willem had been transferred. Johannes van Oorschot served as a mayor for many years after the Second World War, so it's impossible that he was the pro-German mayor mentioned in the story. The pro-German mayor Overbeek only came after Willem had been transferred.[62]

In Lutten the family moved into a detached house. Willem always entered through the back and checked if the clogs were arranged neatly.

Inside the village he was seen as an important person, due to his function. The family didn't suffer from hunger, as there were many farms where food could be acquired, but they experienced, among other things, the shooting of trams, when Allied planes attacked the tram that went through the village. Once a bomb fell near the back of the house, which destroyed all the windows. Besides glass everywhere, the giant crater served as a silent witness to the air war that was fought over the Netherlands.

One day a young German soldier was in the house. Upon seeing the children, he asked Willemien if there were more children present and she took her youngest daughter and let the German hold her. He had difficulty controlling his emotions, as he himself had a young child at home. However, Willem was indignant about it, because his wife showed their children to the enemy.[63]

In Lutten Willem helped people in hiding to coupons that were needed to buy food during the rationing. These coupons were hidden in the frame of his bike and could be transferred between Hardenberg and Lutten without anyone becoming suspicious.[64]

Due to a reorganisation of the police Willem came into service of the *Marechaussee* again, whereupon they also reorganised so they had to perform court services such as guarding prisoners. The court services and the *Marechaussee* were separated again on 1 August 1943, so that the police and justice were performed separately.

Meanwhile Willem was stationed in Rotterdam on 15 June 1943 in order to be promoted to sergeant major, *opperwachtmeester,* in the court services. While there a detachment of the court services was send to Havelte in November 1943, because an airfield was established there by labourers of *Organisation Todt.* The ground needed to be levelled for the German fighters that had to protect the *Heimat* against Allied bombers. In a hotel in Wapserveen Willem established his office and became detachment commander.[65]

While stationed there Willem continued to fight his underground struggle against the occupying forces. Due to his function in the court, he had access to the service car and could use it to help people in hiding. This also included helping Allied air personnel that had jumped out of their planes. Because of his uniform he was allowed a certain degree of freedom. The pilots could be assisted over long distances, ranging from 40 to 80 kilometres. Once a journey like this went from Arnhem to Leeuwarden with two Allied pilots. Six or eight pilots were helped in such a way.[66]

He often travelled within the province Overijssel, such as between Havelte – Meppel or Meppel – Zwolle. Some of the people with whom he was in contact included: C.J. van Hurk, J.H. Mensink, K.A. Drosten, all from Meppel; Wiemers, Pite Peer, Oom Willem, Beernink from Zwolle; A. Sportel, H. Schuurman from Slagharen.[67]

One of these travels has been documented. Together with Gerrit de Jonge, a boy that was hiding in the region of Rotterdam and wished to return home, Willem went to Hoogeveen. Gerrit wrote down his experiences:

> At Broekroelofs I was hospitably received, and we discussed how I could travel as safely as possible. As if it had to be that way, on Monday constable Sebel from Lutten was at the door [in Rotterdam. He came there more often]. He needed to travel back to Assen on Wednesday. I was able to travel with him to Hoogeveen. If something happened along the way, he had to pretend to 'fetch' me. He even had handcuffs with him. (I also had a forged identity card in my pocket). That Wednesday (dankdag [*a Protestant celebration on the first Wednesday of November*] we boarded the mailcarriage of the N.S. [*Nationale Spoorwegen, National Railways*], in the direction of Overijssel. Directly after Zwolle there was another incident. The train stopped suddenly... A truck with rubble had stopped on the crossing. The driver could jump out just in time, but the car was in ruins! Everything went smoothly until Hoogeveen and I arrived safely in Lutten [*to my family*].[68]

After that Gerrit de Jonge stayed at home, although it would be another year and a half before the Liberation.

Airfield Havelte was attacked several times. Twice it was machine-gunned by Allied fighters. Later the airfield became a target for Allied bombers in support of Operation Market Garden. According to the plan Allied paratroopers were dropped in September forming a corridor all the way to Arnhem through which the Allies could enter Germany, although this failed eventually. At the same time the railway strike started in support of the landings. Train personnel hid *en masse* to prevent them from helping the occupying forces. Underground preparations were made to help them acquire food and other supplies. Due to the damage that the airfield took in support of Operation Market Garden, it was unusable for the remainder of the war.

Because of the Allied advances the German occupying powers decided to reposition part of their police forces. The collaborating police in Nijmegen was moved to Zwolle. At the same time Willem was stationed in Zwolle as well, because establishing the airfield at Havelte had been aborted. He took residence in the *Marechaussee* barracks at the Mappelerstraatweg and operated under the alias 'Harry'.[69]

## *In the Dominican monastery*

On 19 March 1945 Willem was supposed to go to Groningen to deliver a message. However, because his bike was broken, he decided to wait for it to be repaired and visit the railroad employee Gerhardus Alferink. Willem's father-in-law was in hiding, because he worked for the railroad services, and Willem wished to collect his salary. The 54-year-old Alferink was a train conductor and helped with the continued payment of the wages of hidden train personnel. The money was delivered in banknotes and distributed further by Alferink or couriers.[70]

Alferink wasn't at home, but working at the Dominican monastery, from where aid was sent to the starving provinces of Holland. Father van Rijn had started the action at the beginning of 1945 to get provisions to the western parts of the Netherlands. Willem decided to visit Alferink there.

Alferink and Willem were talking in a hallway that gave entrance to the offices further on. In these offices police officers, who had fled from Nijmegen, took up residence. Captain-adjutant Kuik was one of them and responsible for affairs concerning the *Marechausse* barracks at the Meppelerstraatweg. Together with *hoofdwachtmeester,* sergeant major, Houwert, he walked by when Willem and Alferink were talking. Willem, dressed in his uniform, greeted them.

Kuik wondered why a bailiff was in the monastery and ordered Houwert to fetch him. While Willem went to meet them, Alferink continued his work. After fifteen minutes Alferink was also brought

# THE FIVE MEN AND THEIR FAMILIES

The postwar ID of Gerhardus Alferink, 1945. (*Alferink family archive*)

to Kuik by Houwert. When they walked together, Houwert said: 'It's not about [you, but] about Sebel.' Kuik had discovered that Willem was in possession of the retirement papers of his father-in-law. This was strange, because his father-in-law was in hiding and couldn't be paid at all.[71]

As soon as Alferink entered the room, Willem had to leave it and was put under guard outside in the hallway. Kuik started questioning Alferink: 'What did that guy want with you?' Alferink replied that Willem had come to ask about the process surrounding his father-in-law's retirement. Kuik then said: 'You're lying. How often has that guy visited you?' 'Twice,' Alferink lied. Willem had come more often, but then it was at Alferink's home in the Celestraat.[72]

Again, Kuik said that it was a lie and ordered Alferink to the hall, where he had to wait with Willem. At the same time Kuik phoned to a superior that 'in the Domincan monastery there was a bailiff, who wasn't at his station and who was involved with money and railway personnel.'[73] The superior promptly informed the *Sicherheitspolizei* and the two men were arrested and brought to the *Dienststelle* of the SD at the Van Nahuysplein. From there they were brought to the *Huis van bewaring*.[74]

The arrest of Willem Sebel was the result of unlucky coincidences. If he hadn't gone to the monastery in uniform, then Kuik would not have recognized him or if Kuik had arrived a few minutes later, Willem would not have been arrested and locked up.

## Berend Jan IJzerman

*Dancing teacher*

Berend Jan IJzerman was born on 14 January 1911 in Kampen, the son of Willem IJzerman and Femmigje Smit. He was named after his grandfather, while his younger brother and sisters were named after other grandparents. He passed the eight classes of primary education. On 16 February 1931 he was called up for conscription with number 115. Berend served in the 20th Infantry Regiment, stationed in Harderwijk. From the moment he started his training, he was destined to be a heavy machine-gunner.[75]

# THE FIVE MEN AND THEIR FAMILIES

*Above left*: A young Berend IJzerman with his mother and sister Hendrika, ca. 1920. (*IJzerman family archive*)

*Above right*: Berend IJzerman, date unknown. (*IJzerman family archive*)

On 7 March Berend was added to the machine-gun company of the 20th Infantry Regiment. He left with his unit for a shooting exercise at the camp near Harskamp and returned to Harderwijk on 4 July. On 31 July 1931 he was allowed to take his long-term leave.[76]

On 12 September 1935 he was called back for a repeat exercise at the Jan van Nassau barracks in Harderwijk. On the last day he received promotion and was send home on 28 September. He took part in another exercise on 9 September 1937 and again served in Harderwijk for two weeks before being allowed to go home again on 25 September.

That year Berend married Gerritdina Hanekamp, who was, except for a day, a year younger than him. They had two children, a daughter Emmy in 1939 and a son in 1944.[77] The daughter was supposed to be named Femmy, after her grandmother, but Berend didn't like it because several nieces also carried the same name, so Emmy was chosen.

The family lived at the Vingboonsstraat 9 in Kampen and was of the reformed faith. Berend loved to dance and taught other people, making some extra money for his family. Besides that, he liked to fish and joined a local fishing club, *Verzopen dobbertje*, 'drowned floater'. However, if the stories must be believed, it was often 'tipsy floater'.[78]

Besides dancing Berend also loved his children. One day he brought home a blue scooter for little Emmy. It was made at the factory where he worked and had real air tyres, unlike other scooters, which had wooden wheels. She was very proud of it and would wait for her father with it at a chestnut tree in Kampen. Then she would go home with him.

Berend IJzerman and Gerritdina Hanekamp, 1937. (*IJzerman family archive*)

Another time he brought home a little gas stove, also made at the factory, which Emmy played with and which had little pans which could be used to boil potatoes above a small candle.[79]

When the Netherlands mobilized on 29 August 1939 Berend returned to the army. He was attached to the machine-gun company of the 44th Infantry Regiment under the command of Captain David van Hoogstraten, who was born on 3 January 1896. The unit was encamped near the Betuwe and Tiel.[80]

Shortly before midnight on 9 May 1940, there came distressing messages about German movements in the east. The company marched towards Echteld where they found that all positions, guarded by three men, were taken. The fourth section of the company was in an orchard approximately 200 metres north of the station against possible German plane attacks.[81]

At 4.30am there came a message from the battalion commander: 'German troops have crossed the Dutch border.' All positions were brought up to full strength. Later that day, at 8.15pm the order came to march to the Waalline and take up positions there. As soon as it was light the men started fortifying the positions.

On 12 May at 12.30pm, in IJzerdoorn, a message came from the battalion commander. The 4th section of the machinegun company needed to move from the orchard towards a position approximately 300 metres from the third company of the third battalion of the 44th Infantry Regiment. The following day at 3.30am the order came that the men could return to their previous positions. Later that day gunboats came down the Waal.

At 4pm the third section was allocated to another unit and three hours later the unit as a whole had to take up positions elsewhere. At 9.15pm the order came for the entire battalion to march to Everdingen. Once there the company moved to their encampment to the south of the café 'de Hommel'. Four hours later came the order to march to a three-forked road to the south of Hagestein and take up positions. Later the order for the surrender came. On 8 June 1940 Berend was sent home on long-term leave.[82]

## *Department chief at the enamel factory*

During the Second World War Berend worked at the enamel factory H. Berk & Zoon, later known as the Kamper Enamel factory. He went to work by bike and when he returned home, his daughter Emmy was waiting for him at the chestnut tree near the Bovenhaven. Together they went home.

To acquire additional food Berend cycled to the farmers in the vicinity of IJsselmuiden and Emmy went along on the back of the bike. She hid the milk that the two collected from the farmers under her jacket when they cycled home. At the factory Berend had made special bottles with handles that allowed them to be tied to someone and closed off with a cork.[83]

How Berend became involved in the underground organisations or how he met Jan Muller is unknown. Probably his illegal activities started with acquiring food and this evolved further to housing people in hiding. People in hiding at the Vingboonstraat 9 stayed in the attic. Gerrritdina explained to her children they were 'guests'. Sometimes it was a single person, but another time there was a group of four people. At night they went on by bike. After the war, Gerritdina told her children that some of these guests had been Jewish.[84]

The IJzerman-family. Standing (L to R): Berend, Hendrika, Tijmbert, Margje. Sitting, Willem, Femmigje, ca. 1934. (*IJzerman family archive*)

# THE FIVE MEN AND THEIR FAMILIES

## *'You can never know what it's good for'*

At the enamel factory there was growing unrest after it became known that part of the personnel had to move to Germany to work there by the end of 1944. This decision was reversed, however, but the employees needed to work for the *Wehrmacht*. In September 1944 the factory was closed as there were no materials available. Instead the freed workers could be put to use by digging positions along the river IJssel, known as the IJssel Line.[85]

At first Berend wanted to go into hiding. He was anti-German and refused to work for them. However, later he changed his mind and applied. When Gerritdina asked him about it, he explained: 'You can never know what it's good for.'[86]

On 4 October 1944 Berend started as a digger for *Organisation Todt* and was later promoted to supervisor. Gerritdina was quick to notice that something was going on which was unacceptable to the Germans. She warned him about this, because he had to be careful and not do anything that would get him into trouble.[87] But slowly Gerritdina discovered what was going on, as her husband was drawing maps in the evening. When questioned about what he was doing, he explained that he was doing this to prevent getting lost in the trenches. She also knew that this was a lie.

Eventually she discovered that he was using his position to survey the surrounding territory. His true intentions were revealed when he let his wife know that he was busy with sketching the entire IJssel Line. If he had a map, he could draw the line on it.[88] These maps arrived soon afterwards, made available by Emelie Jäger-Wolhoff. Her husband was a Dutch officer and had been transported to Germany. His staff maps had been left behind and she decided to put these to use for the Allies. Berend drew the entire IJssel Line on it and the result was picked up by a British seaplane.[89]

## Johannes Albertus Muller

*Fanatical sportsman and sports teacher*

Johannes 'Jan' Muller was born on 24 May 1890 in Rotterdam, the son of Dirk Muller and Elizabeth Toekar. He grew up in the city and worked there as a warehouseman. He served his conscription in Leiden. During the First World War, starting in 1914, he was mobilized and

# TRAGEDY AND BETRAYAL IN THE DUTCH RESISTANCE

guarded the Dutch borders. While he wasn't in Rotterdam, due to his service, he stayed in contact with his beloved, Maria Hendrika van Wingerden, born on 18 July 1891.⁹⁰ He wrote her letters and postcards, like one from 24 September 1914, which included a picture of himself.

> Hereby I send you a nice picture whereupon you'll find a well-known face. Yesterday I sold a whole crate of [*chocolate*] so that goes quite well. You'll certainly have heard from the [*defence works*] that were made in the fort near Karel. Today we made a march to the fort, but we were not allowed to enter the fort. With loving regards [*from your gentleman*] Jan.⁹¹

They married on 14 July 1915 and had two children, a daughter, Bep in 1919, and a son, Joop in 1927. There had been another daughter, Maria, but she died when she was ten months old.

*Above left*: Jan Muller, ca. 1935. (*Muller family archive*)

*Above right*: Jan and Maria Muller with their daughter Bep in Nederweert, 1938. (*Muller family archive*)

## THE FIVE MEN AND THEIR FAMILIES

In October 1919, when the mobilisation was being concluded, Jan could take his long-term leave. He had risen to the rank of sergeant. Unfortunately, it didn't work out with other jobs and he returned to the army. In March 1920 he joined the corps police force. These troops were established to serve as the police service of the ground forces. Their tasks also included border security and military assistance when necessary. Eventually Jan became involved with the Military Gymnastics and Sports School in Utrecht, where he lived for three years. He was a fanatical sportsman and took part in various competitions.[92] Afterwards he was promoted to sergeant-major instructor and acquired several civilian diplomas, such as Leader of the Dutch Gymnastic Society. In March 1925 he was stationed in Nieuwersluis.

In Loenen, in the vicinity, Jan became a teacher at the sportclub *Wilskracht*, 'Willpower', and became their chairman. Among other things, this included handing out prizes at the competitions. Besides that, he gave swimming lessons and was an honorary member of the fanfare corps. He was good with children and very popular.[93]

Jan wasn't only active on a sports level within the municipality, but also worked on a preventive level. On behalf of several inhabitants he filed a request for funds for the upkeep of a playground. Children in the hamlet Mijnden were in danger if they wanted to play on the playground because they had to cross a dangerous road so in the municipal budget for the year 1928 money was put aside for this.[94] Jan was quite popular in the area; three newspaper articles from local papers give a good opinion of his work which explains why he was so popular with the inhabitants of Nieuwersluis and the surrounding area.

> *30 JUNE 1930 – LOENEN. Fallen into a ditch*
> Yesterday afternoon an accident took place on the Rijksstraatweg near the country estate 'Rupelmonde', which ended exceptionally well. A driver, named Smit, from the Keizer company in Zaandam, was busy picking up a car tyre there, when he fell in a deep muddy ditch along the road by the ejection of a jackscrew. If help had not been available very soon, the young man would have been choked in the mud. Sergeant Major Muller of the police force depot and two servants of the Van Schaik firm here managed to save [*Smit*] from his thorny position with

great difficulty. Sergeant Major Muller provided first aid, provided him with clean clothes and called a doctor. The young man was completely dazed, but all turned out well. He was later transported to Zaandam by car.[95]

**29 SEPTEMBER 1932 - LOENEN. *Motorcycle accident***
A serious accident occurred yesterday morning on the Rijksstraatweg near the country estate 'Vredenhoff' here. Behind the bus of Schiltmeijer a young man, a student in Utrecht, drove his motorcycle in the direction of Utrecht. On the bend he wanted to pass the bus but at this moment a luxury car was coming from the opposite direction. The motorcycle came into contact with the luxury car, as a result of which the student was hurled across the street and suffered a leg fracture. Sergeant Major J.A. Muller of the Depot Police troops was soon on the scene with reed splints. Dr. Posthuma and Sister v. D. Hoeven then provided first aid. The patient was taken by ambulance to a hospital in Amsterdam. The motorcycle was seriously damaged.[96]

**27 NOVEMBER 1933 - Pastor Brouwer drove his car in the Vecht and drowned. Dashing rescue attempts by the police troopers failed.**
A sad accident took place in Nieuwersluis on Saturday afternoon about half past two, in which the Rev. Mr. J.J. Brouwer, pastor of the parish Loenersloot, died. At the aforementioned time, the men in the Police Depot in Nieuwersluis heard cries of fear and for help, and they hurried to the Vechtshore, where Father Brouwer's car was barely visible. Sergeant Major J. A. Muller jumped in with the troopers De Vries, v.d. Linden and Oude Hilbrink, the soldier de Leeuw and the citizen Krachting, fully dressed in the water, and they groped around to help the drowning man. They went into ice-cold water three times, but rescue work was made even more difficult by the high Vechtlevel. Stiffened by the cold, they finally tried again but all their work had been in vain. Then one of them jumped again into the Vecht, and with great difficulty he finally succeeded

in carrying the remains of Father Brouwer ashore. In the meantime, many interested people had arrived at the scene of the accident. Dr. L L. Posthuma van Loenen was also present and applied artificial respiration, which had already been performed by Mrs. Ingenhoes, who was there with her husband, owner of hotel 'De Kampioen' on the Vechtbrug, when they saw the car driving in the Vecht to their horror. Despite everything, the casualty couldn't be revived.[97]

At that time the River Vecht caused the surrounding inhabitants many problems. Jan and his policetroopers in Nieuwersluis were ready to help. This was also the case in November 1930 as a newspaper article described:

> ***The alarming high Vechtlevel – Nieuwersluis***
> In connection with the particularly high water level of the Vecht, which rose yesterday evening to 68 [*cm above N.A.P., Amsterdam Ordnance Datum*], the Police Forces Depot was prepared to provide assistance as soon as it was requested. Captain Vermeulen waited until 3am to see if help would be needed. However, the request for assistance came [*this morning*] at 10am, when the Vecht had risen to 74 [*cm above N.A.P., Amsterdam Ordnance Datum*]. Then help was urgently needed. About 25 men, led by Sergeant-Major Muller, went to the Mijndense dijk, which again turned out to be the most threatened point. The water was already rippling over the dike and pouring into the houses. There is a lot of work going on with sandbags and to lay clay dams. At various points in the Dorpsstraat, the water flowed over the Rijksstraatweg, and the flood cannot drain the sewers so dams will also be laid there. The water penetrated into the homes of many residents on this road. As Captain Vermeulen informed us, if the level continues to rise today, the entire depot of 100 troops will go out during the day to provide assistance.[98]

Luckily, through the actions of Jan and his troops, a breach of the dyke had been prevented and on 22 November 1930 Sergeant Major

# TRAGEDY AND BETRAYAL IN THE DUTCH RESISTANCE

Jan Muller was decorated with the Order of Orange-Nassau, with the rank of Knight. The medal was awarded in front of all the police troopers of Nieuwersluis. Captain Vermeulen handed out the medal, while the mayor of Loosdrecht, Q.J. van Swinderen, gave a speech. The Orange Association, a club associated with the local organization of Kings- or Queensday, and the Iceclub showed their support by sending flowers. After the ceremony the festivities were continued in the non-commissioned officers' canteen.[99]

Later a memorial stone was presented to be placed in the Vecht pumping station, which was built to control the flooding in the river. Jan was one of the men present. A special speaker at this occasion was the engineer Anton Mussert, who was at that time working for the

Johannes Muller is decorated with the Order of Oranje-Nassau, 1930. (*Muller family archive*)

## THE FIVE MEN AND THEIR FAMILIES

*Provinciale Waterstaat,* an organization that was responsible for water management, in Utrecht. That same year he would also establish the *Nationaal Socialistische Beweging,* the National Socialist Movement.[100]

At the time Jan was continuing his struggle against the water, he became treasurer at the local Police-Rescuebrigade in Het Gooi and Utrecht. This society was established in 1936 and taught their members how to save drowning people and perform first aid.[101]

Jan also continued his exercises and managed to win several prizes. On 2 May 1932 he came third at a police fencing competition. This wasn't the first medal he would win. Amongst others he was awarded the medal for twenty-four years of faithful service, the Cross for the Four Day Marches, a marching event where the participants had to walk a certain distance every day for the duration of four days, a NOC-medal for passing several sport tests, awarded by the Dutch Olympic Committee, and the mobilization cross for the period 1914-1918. The medal for twenty-four years of faithful service was a big event when Jan received flowers and fruit baskets from the inhabitants, while the Loenen fanfarecorps gave him a serenade. The gymnastics club 'Wilskracht' gave him a fountain pen holder with inscription and the local swimming club gave him a silver watch and an armband.[102]

As Adolf Hitler rose to power and war seemed to be a possibility the task of the corps police forces changed. The men had started as professional soldiers with a police task, but this was later changed to include the manning of casemates. The task of the corps was expanded and for each casemate there was an average of ten police troopers available to man it around the clock.[103] Jan had been promoted again and became adjutant-NCO instructor. In October 1938 he became the commander of a detachment of police forces in Nederweert, in the province Limburg. He and his men had to guard the bridges and sluices and man six casemates, of which three were on an island. Approximately forty troopers were available. During the mobilization of the Netherlands, the group became a position in the Peel-Raam line and its task consisted of blowing up the bridges, destroying the sluices and manning the cannons.

Jan was the head of the detachment that originally consisted of seventy-one police troopers, but which was reduced to fifty-five men. Among them were five sergeants and forty-nine corporals. To them were added twenty-four soldiers from the first battalion, 30th Infantry Regiment.[104]

The casemates numbered III to V were stationed on an island under the leadership of Sergeant Van Maurik, who was in casemate IV. Sergeant Steemers was in charge of the destruction of objects, which included blowing up the solid bridge and sluice 13. Jan himself was in charge of destroying sluice 15. Per casemate there were five troopers, who had to man the cannon, a Type 5 cannon no.2, and the heavy machine-gun, a Schwarzlose M.08. The only exception was casemate I, which had two machine-guns. The police troopers handled the cannon, while the soldiers from the infantry regiment manned the machine-guns.[105]

Sometimes exercises were held to simulate what would need to be done when the bridges had to be blown up. The expectation was that the enemy would attack from the east. During these exercises it was stated that the bridges didn't need to be actually destroyed or the explosives armed. The question remains to what degree these preparations were effective, as for instance the traffic wasn't allowed to suffer any hindrance from the exercises.[106]

## *War from the east*

The May days of 1940 were difficult for Jan Muller. There was tension and preparations were made. On 7 May all leave was cancelled and the casemates manned. Besides that, preparations were made for the destruction of different objects.[107] The next day the casemates stayed occupied and during the night aeroplanes were detected. In the morning again planes were spotted above the island of Nederweert, where there were three casemates. The tension was rising and three men per casemate were assigned to place obstructions across the Zuid-Willemsvaart, Noordervaart and the canal Wessem-Nederweert. After this had been done, they returned to their positions.[108]

Just after midnight, at 1am on 10 May 1940, German planes came over high, flying towards the west. They formed part of the German *Fall Gelb,* the conquering of the Lower Countries. In the following hour tension was rising. Various messages came in and in the east there were light signals in the air. Two hours later, around 3.30am a message was received that the planned destruction of infrastructure needed to be carried out. This started an hour later when the order was verified.

## THE FIVE MEN AND THEIR FAMILIES

The exercises paid off, because despite various setbacks, the objects were destroyed. A German plane opened fire on a group of police troopers that wanted to blow up a bridge, but there were no casualties. At another group the detonator refused to work and matches and a shortened fuse were used to blow up the bridge. The detonator of another group wasn't working either and this was solved by shooting it with a firearm.[109] The result was that nearly all objects, except for one bridge, were destroyed. This last bridge was kept open for retreating Dutch forces. Measures were taken to prevent unnecessary casualties. Early in the morning civilians were evacuated from their homes. Some thieves used the absence of the occupants to raid their homes.

Later that day, at around 10am, the first retreating Dutch soldiers passed through the village. They were coming from the Maas line and with a ferry at Stokershorst they and their vehicles were put on the other side. Later this ferry was also sunk.[110] A few hours of respite followed, until it was broken at 4.35pm, when Jan received a message from casemate IV, under the command of Sergeant Van Maurik, that a German armoured vehicle had been spotted. The order was given to open fire and shortly afterwards another message came reporting a hit on the vehicle. Again, things were quiet in Nederweert.[111]

Forty-five minutes later there was again combat with the enemy. Casemate V was involved in a firefight with a German cannon, which had been deployed in front of them. The casemate was hit and a wooden building set on fire. There were no Dutch casualties and the Germans retreated towards the east.[112] Around 5pm a casemate was overrun after a short fight with the enemy. The personnel, one sergeant and seven corporals, were taken prisoner. At 6.45pm the last bridge was blown up. It was impossible to head east. Jan left the groups' building and took up a position in Nederweert. A quiet night followed. The machine-guns and cannons were fired by nervous Dutch troops a few times. Jan personally took care that his soldiers were supplied with coffee and bread.

The following day at 6.30pm the order came to fall back towards Boeket, to the west of Nederweert. Jan ordered his troops, which included Sergeant Steemers who was in charge of blowing up the last bridge, to evacuate the casemates, disabling the machine-guns and closing the casemates. At the Catholic Church in Nederweert they gathered to proceed to Boeket, where they linked up with their battalion.[113] As soon as it was dark, the battalion would proceed to Streksel, to the northwest of Nederweert with Jan and his unit serving as the rear-guard. Their task was to maintain contact with the German troops, so that the other soldiers could retreat unhindered.

Jan divided his troops into four groups. The first was under the command of Sergeant Geleijns, the second under Sergeant Bastiaans, the third under Sergeant Van Maurik and the last, Sergeant Steemers. Their task was difficult, as the troops lacked heavy weapons.[114] Soon it became obvious that retreating further was impossible due to the German manoeuvres, as became apparent by incoming messages. Jan's detachment was instead used for the protection of the battalion. In the meantime, German patrols were spotted. Firefights broke out, but the Germans swiftly retreated.

That night, from 11 to 12 May, there was a light sky, not due to natural causes, but because of human actions. Light signals were sent up in the surrounding areas. Planes dropped light parachutes that illuminated everything on their journey downwards. In the area surrounding Streksel a forest fire had erupted. At the same time there were talks of surrender.

At around 4am the order was received to gather and to surrender to the enemy. At a roll call, twenty minutes later, it became obvious that Sergeant Steemers and eight corporals were missing. Sergeant Steemers, who lived in Nederweert, had without permission changed into civilian clothes and left. He had recommended a few corporals to detach themselves from their units and to continue the struggle with other detachments but the corporals were captured by the Germans near Someren, to the north of Nederweert.[115]

Meanwhile Jan requested permission from the commander to return to Nederweert. There were a lot of soldiers present and the police forces could be used to prevent irregularities. After being allowed to go, Jan established himself in the Catholic girls' school in Nederweert. From there patrols were send into the village. Many broken shop windows were silent witnesses of the destruction of the war. Loitering soldiers were stopped and escorted towards their units in Boeket.

At 4pm when Jan went to check with the battalion in Boeket, it appeared that German troops were already present. In front of the assembled battalion stood a German officer who ordered Jan to return to his unit. Afterwards the battalion was marched to Someren by the Germans.[116]

## THE FIVE MEN AND THEIR FAMILIES

Back in Nederweert Jan ordered his police troopers to proceed with patrolling and keeping the peace; plundering had to be prevented. The white flag was flying from the Catholic Church tower to show that it wasn't allowed to fire on the Germans.

At 6.15pm a German officer arrived with approximately thirty men at the Catholic girls' school. At the same time a patrol of police troopers returned with an *Oberstleutnant,* a high ranking German officer, who was found in the vicinity of sluice 15. A remarkable event took place, which Jan described as follows:

> After talking back and forth, presumably they see us as civil police, I get permission to stay in Nederweert. I can move into my group building again and have to keep guarding against disturbances. We are allowed to keep the pistols and klewangs [*a type of cutlass*], the carbines must be returned to Boeket.[117]

The next day various civilians returned, curious to see what had passed. It was difficult to maintain control and the German commander in Weert gave permission to Jan to let the population return, which had moved to Someren or Leverooij.[118]

When the police forces took over the building from the German troops again, it turned out to be a mess. The Germans had entered the premises by force. The rear door of the cellar was broken with violence and the wooden frame destroyed. The lock on the gate had been forced and needed to be repaired. Soldiers were still sleeping on the floor. Some lights were broken, as were wardrobes and doors. Repairs and a thorough cleaning followed. Personal objects had also disappeared, such as seven plates and a coffee jar. However, later it was discovered that these objects were loaned to a German soldier by Jan Muller.

However, Jan and his men came through the Battle of the Netherlands in good order. There were no casualties among the soldiers. Jan had a high regard for Sergeant Van Maurik, who had behaved excellently, although the same could not be said about Sergeant Steemers. Casemate IV and V had fired approximately a hundred shells, while casemate I had fired only six.

## Resistance and Arbeitseinsatz

On 4 July 1940 a message came from Colonel J.T. Heins, the commander of the corps police forces. The police troops wouldn't all be placed with the civilian police, as several members of the unit had been involved in demonstrations against the occupying forces throughout the country. Instead, *'the appropriate members* [of the police forces] *would all still find a place in the police services.'*[119] The police troops were allowed to make their preferred station known, but there was no guarantee they would be placed there.

On 15 July Adjutant Muller was discharged from the army and moved with his family back to Nieuwersluis. Jan followed training to be able to work as a policeman. When in March 1943 the police was organized again, he became involved with the Marechausee (one of four branches of the Netherlands armed forces with military and civilian police duties) in the district Zwolle with the rank of sublieutenant. The family lived in Kampen, at the Boelestraat 25. Jan managed to keep his radio, because he was a policeman, so his house wouldn't be searched.

In 1943 the tide was turning against the German war machine. The battle of Stalingrad had been lost and the Germans were on the retreat. To put more pressure on their forces, there were Allied landings in Sicily. In an attempt to regain the initiative, more German men were mobilized for the front to replace the losses. These freed spaces in factories needed to be filled by foreign men.

Joop, the son of Jan, was at risk of being put to work for the Germans through the *Arbeitseinsatz*. He decided to go into hiding in the Noordoostpolder, newly established land in the IJssel lake that had been drained, in the vicinity of Overijssel. Here he helped his father with courier services or other assistance. Once Joop wanted to drag a dead British pilot out of the water, who had been shot down. The corpse was bloated and rotting and when they got the body out of the reeds, an eel came out of the man's nose.[120]

In the second half of 1944 various raids were carried out to gather labourers for German factories, which included a big one in Rotterdam on 10 and 11 November when 50,000 young men from Rotterdam were transported through Kampen and Zwolle towards Germany. Jan managed to free a few of them and even let them stay at his home, before they proceeded elsewhere. He also helped shot down Allied air personnel

## THE FIVE MEN AND THEIR FAMILIES

Jan and Maria Muller with their son Joop, 1942. (*Muller family archive*)

and was involved in the 'Rolls Royce line', with Berend IJzerman.[121] The Rolls Royce line was an illegal connection service, which also performed messenger services. Messages from the western provinces could be passed on to the northern provinces. Jan was the link from Elburg through Zwolle to Zwartsluis. Joop, his son also helped.[122]

In Kampen Jan was in contact with Mrs Jäger-Wolhoff and Berend IJzerman. Together they co-operated to create a correct representation of the IJssel line to pass on to the Allies. Berend drew the maps, which Jäger-Wolhoff had left over from her husband, who gave them to Jan Muller. Jan took care that these maps were handed over to the Allies, by letting them be picked up by British seaplanes from an unknown location.[123]

Despite the Second World War Jan continued his exercises. He even went to sabre and fencing competitions and on 7 July 1944 he came fifth at one of them.

## Jacob Lijs

*V-mann in the Resistance*
Danger was always present, because the *Sicherheitsdienst* was tracking down the members of underground organisations or those involved in

# TRAGEDY AND BETRAYAL IN THE DUTCH RESISTANCE

the Resistance. One of the people who helped the SD was Jacob Lijs, born on 3 June 1903. In December 1944 he returned to Kampen.

Lijs had wandered around for a while and returned home to his mother. In 1928 he had returned from Indonesia and became addicted to morphine. After his return, he became involved in Nazi-groupings, such as the anti-Semitic Rappart-Party. The National-Socialistic Dutch Labour Party was divided into three groups, of which was one led by Ernst Herman Ridder of Rappard. *Ridder* is a Dutch title, similar to knight.[124]

Lijs tried to work as a magnetizer and as an artist but he failed to supply his addiction and by the end of 1943 he was apprehended for the theft of morphine and was forced to spend a year in a clinic.[125]

After his return to Kampen, Lijs asked the NSB-mayor Edward Sandberg for protection against raids and to be freed from work for *Organisation Todt*. Lijs himself was, like him, also a Nazi. According to Sandberg this was indeed possible, but on the condition that he started working as an informant for the Germans. Lijs agreed to this and tried to style himself as an anti-German to the outside world, while still operating as a *V-mann,* a trusted person for the Germans. Lijs was even given a gun by the SD.

Mayor Sandberg and Lijs after the liberation of Kampen, ca. 1945. (*Stadsarchief Kampen*)

## THE FIVE MEN AND THEIR FAMILIES

A successful case that Lijs brought forward was made against a German deserter, who had spent three months in hiding in the Netherlands pretending to be a Dutchman. He was dressed in civilian clothes, in possession of forged documents and probably received the death penalty after Lijs reported him to the SD.[126]

Strangely enough the German organizations weren't impressed with Lijs' work, although because of him several people lost their lives. This was because Lijs also reported cases which entailed little of value or where the occupying forces behaved brutally against innocent people.[127]

Lijs wasn't alone, but had several people working under him. One of those was NSB-member and magician Albert Gort. Gort himself was also involved in the struggle against the Resistance, because he escorted people that had attempted to evade the *Arbeitseinsatz,* but had been captured, from Kampen to Zwolle. Previously this had been done by members of the SD, later by the police in Kampen, and eventually by Gort, because the SD and the police lacked the manpower to perform these duties or refused to do them.[128]

Lijs and Gort were often seen together and it's possible that through Lijs Gort also worked for the SD. Lijs received the identification sign 'J', which he could use to make himself known in communications. Later this was changed to 'J3'. Possibly the 'J' was derived from the name 'Janssen', which Lijs used to make himself known to Mayor Sandberg. There were also plans made by Joseph Rauch, the head of the SD in Zwolle, to arrest Lijs, because he had misled the Germans too often. Fritz Martens, a subordinate of Rauch, prevented this. It didn't help Lijs's reputation that he regularly lied to the Germans to get money for drugs.[129]

Lijs and Gort came into contact when Lijs dropped by Gort's house and introduced himself with another name, Janssen, whereupon Gort replied: 'Everyone calls themselves Janssen, but if I look at you like that, you can be a brother of the coal trader Lijs from Kampen.' Lijs admitted this and asked: 'You're a member of the NSB and a magician?' When Gort confirmed this, the two started talking about magic shows.[130] Due to the interest that Lijs had into this subject, they became friends. Once Lijs told that he collected information for the SD and in the conversation that followed Gort said he wished to do the same, although Gort denied this after the war.

In February 1945 Lijs was arrested during a raid, but was freed due to the interference of the SD in Zwolle and the NSB-mayor Sandberg. Not only did Lijs get free, but also all the other men that were captured. This was done to prevent arousing any suspicion.[131]

A few days later Lijs was in the train to Zwolle, just like Gort, who sat in the same carriage. In the train there were people working for *Organisation Todt* and during the journey someone asked Lijs if they could speak in private. The man knew that Lijs had been arrested a few days previously.[132] The unknown man identified himself as Berend IJzerman and he recommended Lijs to go into hiding as the Germans could arrest him again. In conversation, the name of Mrs Jäger-Wolhoff came up and Lijs wanted to visit her himself in order to find out more about his own arrest. Lijs must have been surprised by this information from Berend IJzerman, as people suspected he was a sympathizer of the NSB.

Emelie Jäger-Wolhoff lived at the Galléstraat, which is currently called the Apeldoornschestraat, together with her daughter, after her own house had been claimed by the Germans. The original owner, a railroad worker, had gone into hiding, which meant she could move in. Emelie's husband had been sent to Germany as a prisoner-of-war.

On Saturday, 24 February 1945, Lijs decided to visit her. Because he was the brother of the coal trader, he could enter her home and pretended to be an illegal worker. The two started talking and Lijs managed to gain her trust by pretending to be an 'Intelligence Service Agent'. He could convince her of his intentions, because he had spoken to Berend before. He went further, claiming that the maps that she had wouldn't reach their intended target through the usual channels. However, he could take care of it. It was agreed that Lijs could return later to discuss this with the person that drew the maps.

After Lijs had left Emelie Jäger-Wolhoff's house, he went to the SD in Zwolle, where he reported his discovery to Fritz Martens. Lijs had found an espionage case. He explained that he had pretended to be a spy for the British and that Mrs Jäger-Wolhoff needed to be arrested the next day, because she possessed a map with the defence works of Zwolle on it. Martens disagreed with this and told Lijs to gather more evidence before he would do anything.[133]

During a later visit, on Sunday evening 25 February 1945, Lijs met Mrs Jäger-Wolhoff again. Gort was waiting outside, hiding in the dark in

## THE FIVE MEN AND THEIR FAMILIES

case something went wrong. Previously he and Lijs agreed that if there was trouble, Lijs would throw a flowerpot through the window.[134]

Mrs Jäger-Wolhoff told her daughter to get Berend IJzerman, whom Lijs had met before in the train. He took a partially filled map with him. Despite the previous contact Berend was doubtful about Lijs and asked him for proof that he really was an 'Intelligence Service Agent'. Lijs countered by asking if Berend thought that he walked around with visiting cards with his profession written on it in his pockets. Berend had to trust him, and if he didn't wish to do so, he was free to take his drawings elsewhere. This managed to convince Berend, who revealed the maps that he had brought along. A few positions were marked on it and he added several more to this.

During the conversation that followed, Mrs Jäger-Wolhoff mentioned that she gave these maps to a certain 'Mulder' in Kampen, who made sure that they reached the Allies. Afterwards Lijs hid the maps on his body and pretended to be careful. It was already after curfew when he took his bike and left.

Lijs didn't hand over these maps to the Allies, but to the German SD. In Zwolle Fritz Martens was ordered by Rauch, his superior, to go to Kampen and pick up the maps that were in the possession of Lijs. Martens left by car at around 10.30pm and returned to Zwolle afterwards to hand them over to Rauch. The maps were checked first as Lijs wasn't fully trusted. After a German pioneer officer verified that the map showed an accurate layout of the trenches, flak, grenade launchers in the surrounding area of Zwolle, the decision to arrest the people involved was made.

The next day, Monday, 26 February 1945, the Germans and their Dutch collaborators held a meeting in a building on the Vloeddijk in Kampen, where various people were present to discuss what would be known as 'the Kamper espionage case'. Among others present were: Bartels, Cieraad, Mönnich, Lijs and Gort. Bartels wanted to know who this so-called 'Mulder' was. There upon it was proposed that 'Mulder' could be Jan Muller, the sub-lieutenant of the police that lived in south Kampen.[135]

That same Monday Berend had received a message that he had to report to the bureau of *Organisation Todt* in Zwolle. Afterwards he was arrested at his work and was found to be in possession of fatal evidence – a map of the German positions around Hattem. That same

*Above left*: Walter Bartels, ca. 1946. (*National Archives*)

*Above right*: Dick Cieraad, ca. 1946. (*National Archives*)

afternoon a thorough house search was done by members of the NSB and Germans at the IJzerman residence to find incriminating evidence. Even the baby was taken out of his crib so they could search it. The German officer apologized for the behaviour of the collaborators afterwards. During the house search no implicating evidence was found, but various things were taken away, such as Berend's helmet that hung on a peg near the door. Probably the NSB-members felt betrayed by Berend IJzerman, because they thought he was a sympathizer.[136]

Jan Muller was arrested in his own home by the Germans. Emelie Jäger-Wolhoff was also arrested, as was her daughter later on. Together they were brought to the *Huis van Bewaring* in Zwolle.

Berend IJzerman, Jan Muller, Jäger-Wolhoff and her daugther, were all arrested because of Lijs's actions. The person they had trusted, betrayed them. Lijs received 300 guilders from Rauch for the information that he had supplied.

# Chapter 3

# In the *Huis van Bewaring*

## *Brought together*

Although the five men were arrested at separate times, they were brought together in the prison called *Huis van Bewaring* in Zwolle, located in the centre of town. Berend IJzerman and Jan Muller were arrested on 26 February. Hermanus Bosch and Wilhelmus van Dijk were brought in on 18 March. Willem Sebel was detained on 19 March.

During the last couple of months, the *Huis van Bewaring* had become quite crowded. It became so full that common criminals had been housed elsewhere since 9 October 1944 leaving only Resistance people and illegal workers. This was partially the result of a beating that the underground organisations in Overijssel had taken, because the *Sicherheitsdienst* had acquired a lot of information about the illegal network. The SD managed to do this through the notebook of Henk Beernink, which had been discovered on his body and contained records from illegal activities. To add to this, there had been information from collaborators and statements derived from the interrogation of people involved in the Resistance or illegal activities. Almost up to the liberation of Zwolle, the SD continued to do its work.

The result of this was that the cells kept getting filled. Willem Sebel, Gerhardus Alferink, Wilhelmus van Dijk and Thijs Brouwer were all put in the same cell, called Woman 4, with fifteen others. Among them was the informant Nicolaas Polderman, born on 18 July 1925 in Rotterdam, who supplied the Germans with information. He wanted to know from everyone why they were arrested. Besides that, there was a member of the NSB, De Klerk. Warnings were given by the Dutch guards when people were being brought into the cells. One fellow detainee, Laurens Bakker, was told by a Dutch jailer: 'There's treason. You'll find friend and foes in the cell. Be careful of what you say.' Little was spoken in the cell, except about the food. Was it sauerkraut or sour white cabbage they ate?[1]

When the SD interrogated their prisoners they used threats and promises. If the members of the illegal organizations or the Resistance co-operated, they would certainly benefit from it. However, if the Dutchmen weren't co-operative, they were threatened with the death sentence or that their homes would be destroyed with grenades.

The inmates knew that as soon as the order 'Get dressed quickly. Take nothing with you!' was given, their time in prison was up. They wouldn't be brought to another prison or return after an interrogation. Only those that would be executed received this order.[2]

On 29 March a group had already been picked up at the jail and brought away. Among them was the police captain Hendrik Bannink, who was known in Zwolle for his illegal activities. Another man who would be executed was the mechanic Johan Langkamp, born on 27 March 1908, married to Hendrika Tempelman and the father of three sons. He was arrested near the end of February.

Langkamp was also a member of 'De Groene', just like Wilhelmus van Dijk. Langkamp had sheltered the Jewish girl Henny Zeehandelaar for a while, offered help to other Jewish or wanted persons, including

Johan Langkamp with his family. (*Langkamp family archive*)

## IN THE *HUIS VAN BEWARING*

Guillette Douwes, Regina, Henny and Henriëtte Zeehandelaar, and was involved in armed Resistance. With others he hid weapons in transformer stations, where high voltage was changed into low voltage, which Langkamp could do through his work for the IJsselcentrale, a power station. The Germans didn't search in these transformer stations, due to the risk of electric shock.

He was in the same cell as Wilhelmus van Dijk and Willem Sebel and gave a note to Polderman, intended for his wife, about weapons and uniforms at their house. Besides that, Langkamp was mentioned in Beernink's notebook. Langkamp saw how Beernik was shot when Beernink was arrested.[3] On 29 March 1945 Langkamp and Bannink left the *Huis van Bewaring* at 3.35am and at 10am word went around that the execution had taken place.[4]

However, an arrest did not automatically mean the death sentence. Every case had a *Sachbearbeiter*, a case worker, and for Hermanus, Willem and Wilhelmus, this was Walter Bartels. Fritz Martens was appointed in the case of Berend IJzerman and Jan Muller, but he received help from Bartels.

Martens was a 45-year-old former teacher. First he had served with the *Wehrmacht,* but later in December 1944 he was transferred to the *Feldgendarmerie* in Kampen. Here he also met the collaborator Lijs. Later, on 15 February 1945, he was transferred to the SD in Zwolle.[5]

The 39-year old *SS-Untersturhführer* Bartels, who had previously been a barber, was transferred to Zwolle in September 1944, after previously serving in The Hague. He worked together with 39-year-old Willy Mönnich, who was in Zwolle to combat communist organisations, but, in his own words, because 'there wasn't a lot to do in this field in Zwolle, I was added to the *Untersturmfüher* Bartels'. Another worker was the Dutchman Cieraad, who was used for various tasks.[6]

There were a few possible sentences for the prisoners. They could receive the death penalty, become a *Todeskandidate* (condemned man) and eventually be executed. They could receive a lighter punishment and be send to a camp in Germany or put to work for the Germans. Lastly the prisoner could also be released. If the person was placed on the death list, which was often the case with severe crimes, it was a matter of time before they would be executed, as they were often used for reprisals.

# TRAGEDY AND BETRAYAL IN THE DUTCH RESISTANCE

After preparing the list for the executions, where Bartels was assisted by Cieraad and Mönnich, the list was sent to Karl Schöngarth, the commander of the *Sicherheitspolizei* and the SD in the Netherlands, who confirmed it and send it back. Illegal workers or members of the Resistance who confessed their crimes were put on this list, those whose guilt was proven, such as through an informant or a fellow prisoner, as well as those that refused to talk, despite condemning evidence.[7]

For reprisals people were chosen who were already captured and hostile to the German regime. They were just sitting in camps, police bureaus or in prisons. For the Germans this meant that they liquidated enemies of their regime rather than keeping them in prison. If random civilians were chosen, the risk was that it would cause more hostility among the Dutch population. The family members and friends of the executed person could join the Resistance or an illegal organization to avenge them.

After *Höhere SS- und Polizeiführer* Hanns Rauter, the highest representative of the SS in the Netherlands, was wounded during the attack at the Woeste Hoeve on the night of 6/7 March 1945, Schöngarth served as his replacement. Schöngarth was born in 1903 in Leipzig and from a young age had extreme-right sympathies. He took part in the German invasion of France in 1940 and from 1 January 1941 he served as the commander of the *SiPo* and SD against the Polish underground. His station was in Cracow, Poland. From May 1943 he served as an officer in the *Waffen-SS* in the fight against partisans in the Balkans. In June 1944 he was stationed in the Netherlands by SS-leader Heinrich Himmler. His task was to make sure that the power of the occupying forces wasn't impaired. This meant that he was responsible for a terror regime in the Netherlands. Towards the end of the war, he could rage for hours in his room, which no one dared enter.[8]

Such an order, which Schöngarth issued, explains the brutal behaviour of the SD during arrests and house searches. In September 1944 the following order was issued:

> Strikes, movements of people in hiding and illegal groups endanger the security of the occupying power. The rest of the family must evacuate houses of arrested illegal persons or houses in which people are in hiding. In order to complicate further use as, for example, a secret overnight

# IN THE *HUIS VAN BEWARING*

*Above left*: Hanns Rauter, date unknown. (*NIOD*)

*Above right*: Karl Schöngarth, date unknown. (*NIOD*)

place of residence or as an illegal courier messaging place, the furniture must be destroyed. This measure must have a deterrent effect at the same time.[9]

The transition from the deliberate demolition of possessions to the stealing of one's property is small, given the shortages that the Germans faced at the end of the war. Rather than destroy what they could use, they started to take the furniture and supplies instead. Of course, the SD in Zwolle also took part in this plundering from civilians.

If a reprisal was ordered, after Schöngarth had taken over from Rauter, he requested a list with some *Todeskandidaten* (condemned men), including their indictment. Schöngarth requested such a list from his subordinate Hans Kolitz, who passed it on to the local head of the SD. In the case of Zwolle this was Joseph Rauch, who acted as commander of the *Einsatzkommando* of the SD in Zwolle. He would then send the list back and, after agreement from Schöngarth, the execution was carried out.

# TRAGEDY AND BETRAYAL IN THE DUTCH RESISTANCE

Hans Kolitz, 1946.
(*National Archives*)

Kolitz was transferred from Dusseldorf to the Netherlands and took up his position on 1 March 1945. As he explained himself, he was

> transferred to the staff of the Sicherheitspolizei Division IV which was then established in Zwolle. I was appointed as the successor of the Regierungsrat Deppner, leader of department IV of the staff of the Befehlshaber der Sicherheitspolizei. The department was the centre where all reports about the Resistance movement entered the Netherlands and were assessed. In this way an overview was obtained of the Resistance in the Netherlands. From here it was arranged which measures had to be taken against the Resistance movement.[10]

He had left his wife and children in Germany where he had previously been a judge in civil cases. He explained his own work in the Netherlands as follows:

> It was my task to judge from the content of the official reports sent by the Dienststelle leaders, which punishment had to

> be applied to the perpetrator, and in particular from the then-present criminal provisions. If an official report meant that the accused had been guilty of a serious crime, such as possession of a weapon or serious sabotage, he would have been sentenced to death by a court of law and thus he had to be executed. [...] In my department I worked on the opposition of the Resistance groups in the Netherlands. Mainly administrative.[11]

Kolitz himself didn't decide who had to be shot during an execution. Schöngarth checked if the sentence was correct on the basis of the official report that was sent along with it. Courts played no role in this process. On 30 July 1944 a *Führerbefehl* (directive) from Adolf Hitler appeared about the 'fight against terrorists and saboteurs in occupied territories', which declared:

> The ever-increasing acts of terrorism and sabotage in the occupied territories, which are increasingly pursued by uniformly guided gangs, force the strictest countermeasures that correspond to the severity of the war that is being forced upon us. Whoever attacks us from behind in the decisive phase of our struggle for existence is not taken into account. I therefore recommend:
>
> I. All acts of violence of non-German citizens in the Occupied Territories against the German Wehrmacht, SS and police and against institutions for the benefit of the aforementioned, are considered terrorist and sabotage acts as follows:
> 1) The troop and every member of the Wehrmacht, SS and police must fight terrorists and saboteurs who find them in the act, immediately and on the spot.
> 2) Anyone arrested later must be transferred to the nearest local office of the SIPO and the SD.
> 3) Supporters, especially women who are not directly involved in combat, must be assigned to work. Children are excluded from this.

# TRAGEDY AND BETRAYAL IN THE DUTCH RESISTANCE

II. The necessary implementing provisions are issued by the Chief of the Oberkommandos der Wehrmacht. He is authorized to make changes and additions to the extent that the necessity of warfare requires this.

This order meant that all courts were cancelled, even ongoing cases. The punishments, as mentioned earlier, included being send to a concentration camp, acquittal, being put to work or the death penalty. People caught red-handed in illegal activities, were to be shot on sight. Those caught later were handed over to the SD or the *SiPo*. Women were put to work for the Germans but children were exempted from these measures.[12]

Some factors also influenced the SD in Zwolle in the decision for capital punishment. Near the end of the war it was impossible to transfer the 'severe cases' out of the combat zone, to prevent them from being liberated by the Allies. Rauch had been prohibited from relocating these people elsewhere. This left him with two options: he could shoot them as soon as the combat operations started in the vicinity of Zwolle, or take them along during the retreat from Zwolle. However, in that case he was personally responsible for them.

Joseph Rauch, date unknown. (*Wolter Noordman*, De vijftien executies)

Crucial and severe cases, including people caught with a firearm or spying, would not end up in Allied hands. To complicate it further, it was unclear how the men of the SD would be used as soon as the fighting started. Would they be frontline troops or would they continue to do their police work? Possibly Rauch made this decision to have his hands free for the coming battle and thus he needed to get rid of the severest cases among the prisoners.[13]

## Wilhelmus and Hendrica van Dijk

After arrival at the *Dienststelle* at the Van Nahuysplein, Wilhelmus van Dijk was interrogated separately, while his wife Hendrica and Thijs Brouwer waited outside the room with a guard. After Wilhelmus had been questioned, the three were transferred by car to the *Huis van Bewaring* guarded by Cieraad. During the ride, he kept a machine-gun aimed at the three prisoners to prevent them from talking or escaping.[14]

While waiting in line to be registered, Wilhelmus whispered to Hendrica that his interrogators wanted to know more about the Allied air personnel. He had said to them that they were Hungerfarers (in Dutch: *Hongertrekkers)*, people who came from West-Netherlands and travelled to the east and north to acquire food. The *Hongerwinter* (Hunger Winter) was nearly over, so it could be a plausible story. If she was questioned, she had to say the same thing.

Wilhelmus and Thijs Brouwer were locked up in the same cell. In it was a room that looked out over the courtyard and thus Wilhelmus and Hendrica could exchange a few words when she was aired and walked by under it. This happened twice per day, once in the morning and once in the evening. Among other things he said to her was that after the interrogation at the *Dienststelle* he wasn't questioned again.[15]

However, this wasn't the only cell where Wilhelmus was incarcerated. For an afternoon he was placed in the same cell as Joop Ester and Herman Meijer, who supplied the SD with information. The idea was that the three of them would exchange information, which the SD could use to track down members of the underground organizations. The three men spoke little and Wilhelmus was put back in his old cell again.[16]

Hendrica still hadn't been heard, even though she had been locked up for several days. Her sister had been freed and the children were looked after.

Once Cieraad came into her common cell and Hendrica asked him: 'Sir, can I speak to you for a moment. I've four small children at home.' Without replying Cieraad slammed the door shut.[17]

She insisted upon being heard and eventually Cieraad agreed. He had also been involved in the arrest and the interrogation provided little information. A few identity cards were shown, whereupon Hendrica was asked if she knew these people. After she had said that she did not, the identity card of her husband was put in front of her. She told Cieraad that she knew him and Cieraad answered: 'Oh, that one is already shot.' Later he contradicted himself, saying that she and Wilhelmus could go free if she gave up the location of Gerrit van Dijk. All she had to do was just come along in the car, point at the residence, and that same evening go home with her husband. Hendrica refused to do this.[18]

In the afternoon of 31 March, she noticed her husband was missing, as she was aired. Brouwer was still in the cell and told her that Wilhelmus had been taken at 6am. His bread was still there and his overcoat and tie still hung in the cell. The day after she wasn't allowed outside and the next day, 2 April, Hendrica was transported to the Westerbork concentration camp.

The Germans knew Wilhelmus was a family member of Gerrit van Dijk, the one they actually wanted to arrest. Through Hendrica they tried to find out where Gerrit was hiding but failed in this attempt. By putting Wilhelmus in another cell, the SD hoped to gain more information, but they got little of value. Wilhelmus himself was in a dangerous position, because at his house a weapon had been found and he would get the death penalty for this. The SD had been well-informed, which is why Wilhelmus and Hendrica were not interrogated very much.

## Hermanus and Gerharda Bosch

Hermanus Bosch was in the same cell as, among others, Hendrik Diele, who was also arrested on 18 March 1945 on suspicion of illegal activities. They didn't know each other well and spoke little about sensitive topics. Hermanus was interrogated once. During this questioning he was shown several pictures of people, including police officer Bannink. The photos were probably taken from identity papers. Hermanus wasn't sure of what attitude to take, because he knew several of the people that he was shown.

Due to his doubt, he eventually admitted that he knew some of the people. Once back in his cell, he had the feeling that he had made a mistake. It had been wrong to admit that he knew some of the people. On 31 March Hermanus was woken and told to get dressed, leaving his overcoat and hat in the cell. He wouldn't return to pick them up.[19]

Meanwhile Gerharda tried to find out what had happened to her husband. At the *Dienststelle* of the SD at the Van Nahuysplein she inquired about Hermanus but received no information and didn't get permission to see him. Yet she managed to discern from the answers that her husband was locked up in the *Huis van Bewaring*. This was also confirmed through the underground movement on 30 March. She was told he was doing well. A day later her husband would be taken away for his execution, but she would only find out later.[20]

Hermanus confessed to knowing people in the underground organizations and probably confirmed German suspicions as they were aware of his illegal activities. He was heard once and possibly the SD knew more than Hermanus thought. Gerharda tried to find out more about her husband, but the German organizations refused to supply information although through illegal channels she did manage to find out more.

## Willem and Willemien Sebel

Willem was disarmed in the presence of Alferink at the *Dienststelle*. From there the two were brought to the *Huis van Bewaring* and put in the same cell as Wilhelmus and Brouwer. There Alferink discovered that Willem Sebel wasn't really called 'Harry'. In the cell were a few other people: Johan Langkamp, Roelof Boltje, Laurens Bakker and Theo Roëll. Bakker was a leading figure in the small space and tried to cheer up everyone. Some of the other prisoners were Dirk Lont, Hendrik Beunk, Harm Pieterman and De Klerk, the NSB-member. A fellow inmate at various times was Nicolaas Polderman.

Polderman shaved the Dutch prisoners and the German guards, which allowed him to be in contact with both sides. Around the middle of March 1945 he worked as a barber at the top floor of the prison, where there were German jailers and the Dutch prison guards weren't allowed. Polderman slept there as well. Sometimes he was allowed to go to other cells, as he was otherwise alone all the time. Polderman sometimes also pretended to be called 'Udio'.

He had a criminal past, which included stealing clothes from his parents' home and selling them elsewhere. On 27 June 1939, when he was 13 years old, he was sentenced to a disciplinary school for handling stolen goods. In 1941 he was again sentenced to a disciplinary school for the same offence; this time he had to stay for seven months. In 1942 he volunteered for the Dutch Waffen-SS for a year. He walked around with the *Wolfsangel,* a symbol that the Nazis had adopted, on his clothing, before his mother took him home. He didn't have to return to the Waffen-SS.

For a while he worked as a digger for the occupying forces and spent a period in concentration camp Amersfoort. This was also used against Polderman to put pressure on him and get him to work for the Germans. In November 1944 he left Rotterdam to go to Zwolle, but a month later he was arrested for possessing a forged identity card. In Zwolle, Bartels convinced 'Udio' to pass along any notes he received to him.

Polderman had certain privileges above other prisoners. He was allowed to smoke and received additional food. Besides that, he pilfered supplies that were smuggled inside. He told stories and managed to earn the trust of several men in the cell. By pretending to be on the side of the Resistance, he received notes that he was supposed to give to the jailer Hendrik Spijkerman, who would smuggle them outside.[21]

During a Sunday afternoon, probably 25 March, Roelof Boltje discovered that Polderman had received notes from Willem Sebel and Johan Langkamp. Boltje warned that Polderman was not to be trusted. Afterwards Langkamp was taken away for interrogation and returned pale. It appeared that the note hadn't gone to his wife, but to Bartels. He had been questioned for three hours, threatened with a bayonet, a pistol and hit with a rifle butt. He had to write a new note with the same words as the one to his wife.

After the interrogation Polderman once looked through the cover in the door. Langkamp noticed this and went over to him to ask where he had left the note. 'I have lost it,' Polderman replied. The brutal realisation that he had been betrayed must have been difficult to sink in. Polderman gave different explanations about the notes, such as saying that he had given them to Hendrik Bannink or to Hendrik Spijkerman.[22]

The note from Langkamp said: *'Dearest wife! You will be surprised that you will receive a letter from me. I am doing well and enjoying good treatment.'* The note further stated that two uniforms were to be handed over to the deliverer of the message. The slip of paper was taken by Cieraad to Langkamp's wife, Hendrika Tempelman, who was waiting for her husband to return. Cieraad confronted her with the message. At first Hendrika didn't trust the situation, as she had never met Cieraad and the other person, who was dressed in a German uniform. Yet both men received the benefit of doubt. She handed over a sack containing a uniform after it had been collected from the neighbours.

She was arrested later, when she was on the road to warn the owner of the uniform she had given away, about the incident. Through a hole in the window Langkamp could see that his wife was taken in. The rest of the time Langkamp read his Bible. When he was taken away for his execution, he shook Alferink's hand and asked cellmate Bakker to think of his children and wife.

In an attempt to get in contact with other people involved in the underground movement, Willem Sebel handed over a note to Polderman, meant for Jan Muller and Hendrik Bannink. It was supposed to contain information about an escape attempt. This letter was also handed to Walter Bartels, who judged that it was proof of Willem's illegal activities, as the three were in contact with each other. Besides that, papers had been discovered which showed that Willem served as a messenger and Bartels knew Willem Sebel had been in hiding.

On 31 March Willem was collected by a Dutch and a German jailer who said that he was probably being taken for a hearing. He was told 'you can leave your coat'. According to Laurens Bakker, Willem wasn't fully aware that he was about to be executed.[23]

## Berend and Gerritdina IJzerman

The day after Berend hadn't returned home, Gerritdina went to Zwolle to get information at the *Dienststelle* (Department) of the SD. Here she was told that her husband had been arrested and was in the *Huis van Bewaring*. Meanwhile Mrs Jäger-Wolhoff and her daughter, as well as Jan Muller, were arrested. A day later a member of the *Sicherheitsdienst, Ooberfeldwebel* Fritz Martens visited the IJzerman residence.

He was involved in the investigation and promised to try to prevent the capital punishment which was usually given for espionage. He wished to know more about what she knew of her husband's doings. She replied that she could tell him little, as her husband didn't speak with her about his illegal activities.

On 10 March Gerritdina got permission from Martens to visit her husband. Martens would be present during the conversation but they weren't allowed to talk about the arrest or anything linked to it. Secret information couldn't be shared and they spoke about other things for the last time.[24]

## Emelie Jäger-Wolhoff

Emelie Jäger-Wolhoff had been captured and incarcerated at the *Huis van Bewaring*. The SD used the situation to ransack her home; silverware, clothes and jewellery disappeared. Even the alarm clock was stolen. Some of her things were taken by the SD, such as her typewriter. Foodstuffs and fuel were also seized by the SD and used for their own purposes.[25]

While she was locked up, she requested if she could get clean underwear. Martens said he wanted to consider it, if she could manage to get it collected at her own house and brought to the *Huis van Bewaring*. According to Martens this wasn't allowed by a superior and her request was refused.

Meanwhile it had become obvious during questioning that Lijs had betrayed her. Although Jäger-Wolhoff at first denied any involvement, she was later shown a statement from Jan Muller after which she also confessed. While she was in prison, she wasn't mistreated or sexually assaulted. Her daughter, who wasn't involved in anything, was also kept for the entire duration of her stay. Together they were put on a transport on 2 April 1945 to go to camp Westerbork.[26]

## Jan and Maria Muller

Jan Muller had made a statement for the Germans, admitting the espionage, but remaining silent about other things he had done.

## IN THE *HUIS VAN BEWARING*

The evidence against him supplied by Lijs was overwhelming. Yet Rauch, the head of the SD in Zwolle, wanted to know to whom Jan was supposed to pass along the maps, but Jan refused to tell this. The confession was incomplete, but it was enough for Bartels. Martens had to wrap up his research, so that Jan and Berend could be executed. Jan, as he told in a conversation on 30 March, was afraid of being executed.[27]

Lijs declared that he could prove that Jan was an illegal worker. He claimed to know that there was a captain in Kampen to whom Jan had given the map. Jan denied this, although he admitted to knowing the captain. Martens didn't tell this to Rauch, to prevent the captain's unnecessary arrest.

Maria Muller was home alone after her husband had been arrested. Her son Joop was in hiding and her daughter Bep wasn't living at home anymore. A few days after the arrest, she received a visit from SD officials. Bartels and Cieraad wanted to know where the two maps from Jan were and the letter from Mrs Jäger-Wolhoff. When Maria repeated several times that she knew nothing about the illegal activities of her husband, Cieraad threatened to deport her to Germany and to throw a hand grenade into her house. However, Maria had no information to share and the two men left empty-handed.[28]

The SD chose another approach and Lijs was sent to the Muller residence. He pretended to be someone from the underground but was distrusted by Maria. While Maria herself claims not to have said anything, Lijs stated she had trusted him. It's possible that Lijs acted under pressure from the Germans, or that he did it to feed his morphine addiction. Regardless, Lijs told the Germans that she had explained to him that she warned another illegal worker, whereupon Maria was arrested by the SD.

In the *Huis van Bewaring* she was again interrogated about the maps and the letter. She kept denying everything, even after she was confronted with Mrs Jäger-Wolhoff, who told the Germans, in the presence of Maria, that she had handed her a letter. This was extremely stressful for Maria as the Germans were relentless in their interrogations. The questioning was often done by Bartels or Martens. Once Martens ordered Maria to be confronted with Lijs to try and gain information from her. Lijs was hesitant to co-operate, but eventually agreed if the Germans pretended he was also a prisoner. So, he was cuffed and treated as a fellow detainee.[29]

During the ploy, Maria was put with her back towards Lijs and she got the impression that Lijs was violently questioned. He groaned loudly, but she didn't understand what questions were asked of him, as she was partially deaf. The whole interrogation had been set-up, in order to put pressure on her. When this happened, Maria was shown a picture of Lijs and asked if she knew him. Maria replied: 'This is a former non-commissioned officer, who knows about everything.'[30]

Other questions that were asked during the interrogation concerned her visit to Mrs Knipmeijer, whose husband was involved in illegal activities and searched by the SD. The SD suspected that Maria had warned her.

In her own statement after the Second World War, Maria stated that she wasn't aware that Lijs worked for the SD, while Martens in his statement claimed that Maria had seen through the ploy immediately and had called Lijs a 'traitor' upon his entry. Lijs defended himself against this by saying that he had been tortured and thus said her name. Martens also claimed that Lijs wasn't really punched during the interrogation, which Lijs denied.

Eventually, on 2 April, she was sent to camp Westerbork where two German female guards took two rings from her. One was her wedding ring, with the date 15-7-15 engraved in it, and the other one a seal ring.

Despite valiant attempts, the fates of the men were sealed during their arrest. Berend and Jan were caught for espionage, which meant the death penalty. Wilhelmus was arrested after a radio, illegal foodstuffs, *Wehrmacht*-tools, a *Wehrmacht*-binocular and a pistol were found as his home. Especially the pistol was condemning, as he would be branded a 'terrorist' and be executed. Willem had been in hiding and was linked to the underground organizations through the note that had been intercepted.

Hermanus is unique, because the weapon in his possession wasn't discovered. Apparently, he confirmed German suspicions by admitting that he knew some people in the underground organizations and for that reason he was made a *Todeskanidate* (liable for execution). It's also possible that a fellow inmate supplied information about Hermanus or that Hermanus refused to co-operate despite the overwhelming evidence.

Hungerfarers at the Meppelerstraatweg, 1944. (*Historisch Centrum Overijssel*)

The first monument at the Meppelerstraatweg, 1945. (*Historisch Centrum Overijssel*)

# Chapter 4

# The Verdict and Westerbork

In the spring of 1945, the parts of the Netherlands still under German control were growing restless. The end of the war was near, and the Resistance were more audacious in their attacks. The railway tracks were destroyed or damaged to hamper German transports. The march of the Allies was in full swing and the Third Reich was collapsing. To accelerate the Allied advance, underground organisations launched various attacks. For example, railways and bridges were blown up.

## *The execution*

Some days before 31 March 1945 an attack blew up the railway between Zwolle and Meppel, the last railroad between East-Netherlands and Germany. The railway bridge across the canal Dedemsvaart was destroyed by an illegal group that involved Daan Querner. They deliberately struck the bridge, because repairing it was difficult.[1]

Reprisal was beyond doubt and a list was prepared with *Todeskandidaten*. Two days before, on 29 March, an execution had already taken place in Wierden. Twenty men, including Hendrik Bannink and Johan Langkamp, were shot.

Five men were chosen for the list. On this list were Berend IJzerman and Jan Muller, in spite of the unfinished investigation, who were guilty of espionage and had to be put to death. On 28 March their execution was confirmed. Bartels had visited Martens around 3pm and said: 'Tomorrow an [execution] takes place and Muller and IJzerman will be there.' Martens claimed that the case wasn't closed yet and that Jan needed to be heard to find out to whom he gave the maps.[2]

A few hours later a message from Bartels came that the two wouldn't be shot yet and that Martens could continue the case.

## THE VERDICT AND WESTERBORK

Jan and Berend avoided the execution in Wierden and on 29 March Jan was questioned by Martens. On 30 March the two men were again placed on the list of *Todeskandidaten* by Bartels. Martens hadn't made a closing statement yet, because Jan had only partially confessed. After Bartels stated that the two men were going to be put in front of a firing squad, Martens changed the date on the official report, by backdating it to two days earlier, so that the men could be executed. The documents were thus falsified.[3]

It is remarkable that Berend and Jan were executed so shortly after they had been taken off the list. The reason for this isn't clear. It could be that Bartels held a personal grudge against one of the men or that Bartels judged espionage more harshly than other crimes. Of course, the decision was influenced by the Allied advance, the two men were not allowed to be taken alive and the SD wanted to have freedom to manoeuvre, without concerning themselves with their prisoners. By shooting them beforehand, the SD soldiers were free to be used on the front. Another motive could be to eliminate as many witnesses as possible, because they might have seen or heard things that could testify against the SD after the war.

*Obersturmführer* Fritz Winter, a 46-year old former teacher, was appointed to oversee the execution. For four years he had been stationed in Brussels with the *Geheime Feldpolize,* but ended up in Zwolle due to the rapid Allied advance after D-Day. An additional officer Friedrich Genczyk was appointed, who had been wounded in the head during the First World War. In 1939 he had been called up for military service. Both men were dressed in grey uniforms and flat caps.[4]

On 30 March Winter was ordered to Rauch for instructions. The place of the execution had been decided, the *Meppelerstraatweg.* This location was chosen because the railway went from Zwolle to Meppel. Fritz Winter got, among other things,

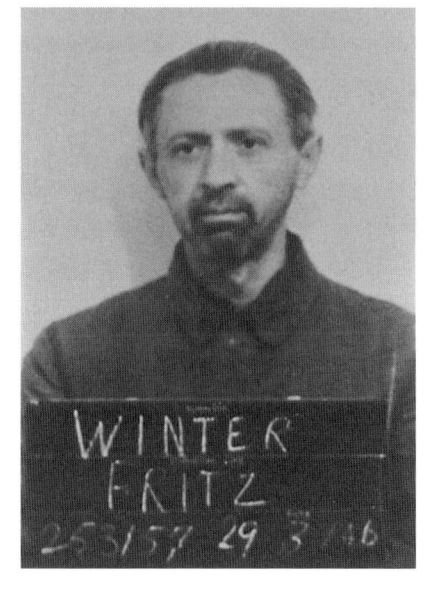

Fritz Winter, 1946. (*National Archives*)

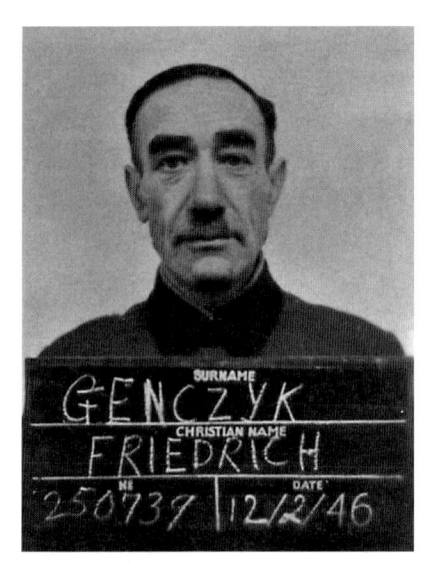

Friedrich Genczyk, 1946. (*National Archives*)

a list of notes about the five men and their committed crimes: weapon possession, espionage and such. A translator was needed to translate the charges and for this Cieraad was chosen. The firing squad would be ready the next day at 6am, consisting of ten men of the *Ordnungspolizei*. The corpses needed to be left behind as a warning to the population of Zwolle.

The next day the prisoners were woken, their names confirmed and the list checked. After everything was correct, their hands were tied and they had to take their places in a bus covered with a camouflage-net. Their possessions were left behind. In the same bus were the men that made up the firing squad. Winter himself was in a personal car with a few other Germans. At the prison Winter had told the officials to remove the prisoners from the registers. Cieraad was present in civilian clothes; he had wanted to experience an execution.

The five Dutchmen knew what was waiting for them. They had heard the same orders before and those men hadn't returned either. They saw the helmeted policemen with their weapons and knew why they had been taken.

The two vehicles stopped at the Meppelerstraatweg. Nearby was the *Marechaussee* Barracks where Willem Sebel had a room. A little further on the Balistraat was where Wilhelmus lived with his family. Three Germans were put on opposite sides of the road to stop the traffic. They had to halt the people and cars at approximately 100 metres distance. Wilhelm Hukriede and Reinhard Stuck halted the flow in the direction of Meppel; Böll in the direction of Zwolle. Stuck stopped the cars on the road and a horse and wagon driven by Johannes Jansen. Böll and Hukriede didn't like to be present at executions. For Böll this was a religious matter, as he was a devout Catholic and, on those grounds, refused to participate in firing squads.[5]

Various people, including Arend Kreder, Hendrik Selhorst, Harm-Jan Otterman, who feared to be put to work for the Germans, Casperus

## THE VERDICT AND WESTERBORK

Tardi, Dini van der Horst and Jan Kamphuis, who were on the Meppelerstraatweg at that time, had to stop and were unintended witnesses to the horrible act. Among the witnesses were also children, like Wim, the son of Harm-Jan, and Andries, the younger brother of Dini, who would spend the rest of their lives with the trauma of that horrific morning. Heimert Oordijk, a roadworker on the way his work in Dalfsen, was cycling on the Meppelerstraatweg and ordered to move on, while these 'saboteurs' were shot.[6]

Wilhelm Hukriede, 1945. (*National Archives*)

Amongst the witnesses were the people on Johannes Jansen's wagon from Oldeneel. That morning Jansen had gone on the road with horse and wagon to bring Hungerfarers (*Hongertrekkers*) from Zwolle to Meppel, so that they wouldn't have to walk that part and could rest a while. Approximately thirty people were on the flat cart that Jansen had borrowed from his neighbour. Jansen's wife hadn't agreed with the decision of her husband to help these people, because she feared that he would be shot by British fighters. Despite her protests, he insisted on helping and thus left that morning in the direction of Meppel and ended up on the Meppelerstraatweg. He, together with his thirty passengers, would be witnesses to what was about to happen.[7]

The five Dutchmen were put on right side of the Meppelerstraatweg between the trees, their hands still tied, while the Germans, like Rudolf Schmidt, stood on the road. Winter read out loud the accusation in German: as a reprisal for blowing up a railway bridge the five men were now to be executed. Cieraad translated this to Dutch. A short moment followed for the men to pray.

Afterwards the firing squad lined up. Half of the men knelt, while the others half stood behind them. Two rifles were aimed at every man. After lining up, the order was given, a volley followed, and all five men fell down.

Winter wanted to be certain that the five men were dead and ordered a subordinate, Erich Hohmann, to give the *coup de grâce*. Hohmann reached for his new pistol, which he had previously test-fired in a ditch. He fired a shot at the heart of one man. The next shot was a misfire. A new pistol was handed to him by Cieraad, but this weapon also refused to shoot. Hohmann stepped backwards and Winter himself used his personal sidearm to fire a round through the head of every executed man.[8]

Erich Hohmann, 1946. (*National Archives*)

The SD officials, the firing squad and others then got into their vehicles and left without posting a guard near the corpses. The bodies were left as a warning to the population of Zwolle. The two cars drove in the direction of Meppel, but at the roundabout turned back to Zwolle. Once back at the *Dienststelle* the Germans had breakfast.

It is remarkable that Erich Hohmann mentioned that he didn't recognize the pistol that was given to him by Cieraad. He saw that it was a 'small calibre' weapon and was certain that Cieraad handed it to him. The same words, 'small calibre' were also used by Hendrica van Dijk to describe the pistol that she and Wilhelmus had hidden at their home. The possibility exists that it was an Allied weapon, which was supplied in a drop, or an old Dutch pistol. Cieraad was present at the arrest of Wilhelmus van Dijk, where a 'small calibre' firearm had been pilfered. The weapon was mentioned in statements but disappeared from the list of confiscated goods.[9]

Weapon possession was mentioned on the list of personal belongings and it was a reason to be sentenced to death. None of the other men had a weapon that had been discovered, besides it would explain why Wilhelmus was on the list. It is plausible that the weapon had been filched by Cieraad, who was then present at Wilhelmus's execution.

## THE VERDICT AND WESTERBORK

The irony is that the weapon which Wilhelmus had thought would keep him safe, was the reason he was condemned to death and was present at his execution.

Winter himself stated, after the Second World War, that he had given the men time to pray, but none of the other people, witnesses or Germans, mention this in their statements. Of course, it was a stressful event and witnesses remember different parts of the same events. At the execution in Wierden people were given time to pray.[10]

The bodies were left behind as an horrific example. Frank Apotheker, a policeman in Zwolle, had been given the task of guarding the bodies until they could be moved. He arrived shortly afterwards, when the SD reported the execution. How many people saw the corpses is unknown. Heimert Oordijk was one of them, when he returned homewards a few hours later. Ank Meliesie-Appelhof, who was a teenager at that time, saw the bodies unexpectedly:[11]

> My grandparents had a bakery shop in the Voorstraat. On Friday, if there was a market, farmers from the local area would go shopping. My grandmother treated them to coffee in the room behind the store. As a result, my father knew many farmers, where we were allowed to get milk. In all weather we cycled to Wijthem, Berkum, Haerst and the Plankenloodsje. My mother had sewn large bags that she wore under her skirts. She put the milk bottles in there, because if a control showed that you had food with you, you would have lost it. During such a trip I once experienced something terrible that I will never forget.
>
> I cycled over the Meppeler[straat]weg, where it was still very rural at the time. The flats and houses that are now there were not yet there. I saw a policeman standing in the distance. At first I wanted to go back because I thought there was a check, but no one was arrested and moreover I only had empty bottles with me. So I drove on and suddenly I saw some corpses on the side of the road. I did not want to look (I had never seen a dead person), but it was as if my eyes were drawn to it. At that time, my future brother-in-law was in jail, and I looked at the shot men one by one. When I cycled back, I made a big detour, because I didn't dare to pass it again. When I got home I was completely upset.[12]

*Above left*: Heimert Oordijk, date unknown. (*Oordijk family archive*)

*Above right*: Rudolf Schmidt, ca. 1945. (*National Archives*)

Around 1.15pm on 31 March 1945, the corpses were brought to the morgue of the cemetery Kranenburg. At 3pm two police officers, Aeldert Sattler and Lammert Hamming arrived, who were tasked with identifying the corpses. Wilhelmus van Dijk was mauled so badly that his neighbour, Sattler, didn't recognize him at first. Willem Sebel was known immediately, the others were identified by their clothes and through pictures.[13]

## *The Women March*

Four of the arrested women, Maria Muller, Emelie Jäger-Wolhoff and her daughter, and Hendrica van Dijk, were transported to Westerbork camp, where they arrived on 2 April. Here they were put to work and experienced the march to the north. During the end of the war, the Germans evacuated part of the camp to keep the women out of Canadian hands.

Since 13 September 1944 no trains had left Westerbork for the east. There were 876 Jews in the camp who cooked for the 116 women that

## THE VERDICT AND WESTERBORK

were brought in. Originally there had been 500 Jews, but Jews discovered in hiding were later brought to the camp, resulting in the higher number. With the Liberation approaching, people could hear cannon fire and Allied planes flew over regularly.

At their arrival at Westerbork camp the women received blue overalls with red numbers at the back. Maria's was 92, Jäger-Wolhoff and her daughter 94 and 95, Hendrica's was 97. Their hair was cut and clogs handed out. The 116 women included illegal workers, couriers and women married to men involved in the underground organizations. They were put to work and needed to split batteries, which made them very dirty, but they were unable to wash.[14]

On the eve of the Liberation there was unrest in the camp. After the original camp guards had left on 10 April, 500 German soldiers were left behind as new reluctant guards. They would leave the coming night. However, they wouldn't leave alone, as they took the 116 women with them. The plan was to march across the Afsluitdijk to North-Holland.

Clothing was distributed to the women to wear over their overalls, so that they wouldn't be recognized as prisoners. They weren't told the destination of the journey. During the roll call, just before leave, the women were waiting in line. It turned out that three women had hidden in the camp. The German commander put all women in a row and threatened to shoot every tenth woman if the women in hiding weren't found. Within fifteen minutes the missing women were discovered and put in their place. At 11pm the group started marching to the north.[15]

The women left in rows of five and were surrounded by their 500 guards. To stay hidden from the Allied airplanes they walked until dawn when they reached the village Peelo. Here they slept in straw at a farm and were given food. The next day, after 6pm, they continued their journey northwards. Because of possible drop-outs, such as the elderly and the sick, horses and carts were found. Now short breaks could be taken by the women walking. However, it also meant that progress slowed down.

The second overnight stay was in the vicinity of the village Vries, in the north of the province Drenthe, from where they left the next day again at 6pm. When the group wanted to continue, a few Allied planes flew over. The German soldiers hid in the ditches, while the women cheered: 'The Tommies! The Tommies!' Angrily the troops ordered that the women weren't allowed to leave their rows anymore. That night the women went with their guards through Groningen. It was raining, the city was full of soldiers and the mood was tense with the impending Liberation.[16]

Around 5.30am, outside Groningen, a short break was granted. The women were given milk by a farmer. The local villagers that saw the ladies come by, understood that they weren't NSB-women, but prisoners. Many of the 116 women were tired and couldn't go on. The German commander decided to abandon a small group and ordered the rest to march on.[17] The remaining group continued their journey. The women were tired and some stumbled onwards, exhausted and hungry; those that fell out were put on carts. To make the situation worse, the food was running out. The last sack had been emptied. The German guards needed to keep what was left for themselves, because due to the Allied advance supplies appeared irregularly.[18]

To prevent encirclement, the column had to march faster. However, this was impossible as the exhausted women needed to be guarded and dragged along. The German commander had to make a choice and had the women line up. However instead of executing them, he let them go. They were freed in the vicinity of Grijpskerk and could, after Canadian soldiers had arrived, return home.

## Shots on the road to Staphorst

The Liberation was approaching, yet in these final weeks there were many casualties. Among them were five men that were executed by the SD in Meppel. This was also part of a reprisal for an attack on a railway bridge between Zwolle and Meppele. The victims were in the SD-prison at the *Stationsweg* in Meppel. The locals called this building *Sing-Sing*. The SD-commander was Paul Thümmel, who previously fought against underground organizations in France. During interrogations he maltreated his prisoners.[19]

However, the danger didn't just come from there. Near the end of February 1945, a girl had arrived in Meppel to be with her boyfriend, who worked for the SD-Meppel. She tried to get housing with her family, the family Uiterwijk, but was rejected due to her NSB-membership so she went to Thümmel to see if something could be arranged. Thümmel knew that members of the Uiterwijk family had been in hiding and decided to search the residence. The head of the family was arrested and a notebook

# THE VERDICT AND WESTERBORK

Johan Stomp, date unknown. (*NIOD*)

was found with the name of baker Huizing and a stamp. Thereupon that house was also searched and a pistol, calibre 7.65mm, was discovered in the bedroom of the baker's assistant Johan Stomp. The baker, his wife and Stomp were arrested.

About the interrogation that Thümmel conducted, he said after the war:

> The interrogations were led by me and during the first hearing of Stomp, he confessed entirely voluntarily and without any coercion, everything he knew about illegality, and he called many names.'[20]

This statement is in stark contrast with what a fellow prisoner reported. Sienna van Essen, a costume maker, was also questioned by Thümmel:

> On 27 February 1945 I was arrested by the SD from Meppel together with Hartholt, who was in hiding with me. [...]

When, during the interrogation, I did not answer their questions to the satisfaction of the gentlemen, they both struck me at the same time and forcefully with an outstretched hand on my head, leaving me deaf for three days. Furthermore, because I did not want to tell them who was the leader of the raid on the Dutch Bank, which had taken place in the *Achterhoek* and in which Hartholt was involved, I was threatened with a dog. This was done on the advice of [...] Jo Habing [from the Dutch *Landwacht*], whom I knew from before. However, when I maintained that I could not name that leader's name, I was taken out of the shed, where Habing was already ready with the dog to release it on me. [...] Practically all the prisoners were mistreated during the interrogation, which we could hear from the cries of pain when they screamed.'[21]

In the afternoon of 3 April, the phone rang at the *Dienststelle* of the SD in Meppel. Hans Kolitz, the subordinate of Schöngarth, called for Thümmel with a special assignment – five men needed to be executed. Did Thümmel have enough men for this? This was answered positively, as later that day, between 5pm and 6pm, there was a secret telex message for Thümmel at the *Befehlshaber der Ordnungspolizei* (Police Commander's Office), also in Meppel. Because the *Dienststelle* of the SD didn't have their own telex machine, it was sent there. Hugo Geigolath was ordered to fetch it and the message was clear: as a reprisal for an attack on the railway between Zwolle and Meppel five men had to be shot who were arrested as terrorists or hostages. They had to be left for three hours at the place of execution after the punishment was carried out. Notices had to make it clear why these men were shot.[22]

The SD in Meppel then discussed further proceedings: which men were eligible to be executed? Finally, a selection was made: Berend Nijenhuis, Cornelis Meijer, Johan Stomp, Hendrik Hartholt and Jan de Boer. Geigolath would lead the firing squad, that consisted of personnel from the SD-Meppel, and two weapons were assigned for every victim.[23]

The notices were prepared that evening at the *Dienststelle* and the SD-personnel were informed. Geigolath went over to the prison where

# THE VERDICT AND WESTERBORK

*Above left*: Jan de Boer, date unknown. (*NIOD*)

*Above right*: Cornelis Meijer, date unknown. (*NIOD*)

*Below left*: Berend Nijenhuis, date unknown. (*NIOD*)

*Below right*: Hendrik Hartholt, date unknown. (*NIOD*)

he informed Knickmeijer, who worked there, that the prisoners had to be ready for collection in the morning. While he explained to Knickmeijer why the men were being taken away, Kickmeijer had to inform the prisoners that they were being transferred. To keep up appearances, they had to pack their possessions properly.[24]

The next morning, 4 April 1945, the prisoners were picked up by Geigolath in a red delivery van, marked with 'J. van Buren' on the side. Afterward the *Dienststelle* was visited, where the SD were picked up. Behind the vehicle drove a car with Thümmel and the execution squad inside. South of Meppel, the vehicles stopped.

Aaltje Plezier, who had been staying in Meppel for some time, was on the road to get food from the local farmers. She heard Dutchmen speaking in the van and was ordered to leave the vicinity.[25]

The road to the north and south was blocked. The prisoners were put between the trees on the eastern side, while on the west side the firing squad took up its position. The line-up, from north to south, was Nijenhuis, Hartholt, Stomp, Meijer and De Boer.[26]

The SD-member Helmuth Detand told the prisoners why they were being shot. Thümmel added to this that 'it was *Krieg* (war), that claimed many human lives and that now they needed to sacrifice their lives.' Someone asked if his life could be spared, but Thümmel rejected this. A short moment of prayer was granted and afterwards Hugo Geigolath gave the order to fire. Four men fell down, but Nijenhuis kept standing. A second volley was needed to take him down. Two shots to the head followed to every Dutchman if they doubted he was dead. Aaltje Plezier heard the shots but was afraid to turn around and look.

Afterwards the notices were put up on the trees in the vicinity. Detand and Thümmel went to the police bureau to inform the police of the execution and to let them guard the corpses for three hours before they could be buried. One member of the SD stayed behind to make sure this was all properly taken care of.[27]

Once back at the *Dienststelle* in Meppel, Thümmel contacted Hans Kolitz to let him know that the execution had been carried out. Aaltje Plezier, who passed the place again 40 minutes later, saw five corpses. Nine days later Meppel was liberated.[28]

It is remarkable that there are a few coincidences between this execution and the one at the Meppelerstraatweg, which suggest that it could have been a single reprisal, carried out in two parts.

## THE VERDICT AND WESTERBORK

The men in Meppel were shot on the way to Zwolle, while the men in Zwolle were shot on the way to Meppel. In both cases it was five men, who weren't sentenced. Both executions were a reprisal for an attack on the railroad between Zwolle-Meppel, although in the case of the Meppelerstraatweg, it was referred to in several ways: an attack on a Red-Cross train, an attack on the railway Zwolle-Meppel and an attack on a railway bridge.

However, there are also a few things that suggest these were separate retaliations, as the dates differ: 31 March and 4 April. On 4 April there was also an execution at the Geldersedijk in Hattem, but this was a separate reprisal. The reason for this is that the railway to the south of Zwolle had been attacked and in this execution six men were shot. It could be a possible retaliation for an attempted attack by Bonno van Dijken and a few others, who were also part of 'De Groene', who tried to blow up the IJsselbridge near the end of the war. Previously, they had struck the railway elsewhere, but this had quickly been repaired.

Strangely enough, during these raids, they noticed that the Germans received unexpected help. When the men walked through the fields and pastures, curious cows followed them. When the men had to hide in bushes or ditches and canals, the cattle went after them. The men were in luck, because during one of these incidents, the German soldiers didn't notice why all the cows were standing at a specific place. They probably all came from the cities, as otherwise they would have known what was happening. Regardless, the strikes against the railway tracks did little damage and instead they resolved to attack the bridge itself, which would be more difficult to repair. During the night, they went there, prepared the explosives and shortly afterwards there was a tremendous explosion. The next day they returned to see the damage. To their disappointment, the bridge was damaged, but still standing. Their strike had failed.[29]

A proper explanation for the later date for the execution on the road to Staphorst is missing. It could be that in the chaos of the last days of the war, as the Third Reich was collapsing, that communications were hampered and that the whole processes took longer to carry out. Maybe Kolitz and Schöngarth hadn't got around to it, as they were busy with other things. Of course, it could still be that the two executions are separate from each other and aren't linked in any way.

*Above*: The Interior Forces during the liberation of Zwolle. On the left is Piet van Dijk, the brother, and at the back, holding the flag, stands Piet van Dijk, the son of Gerrit, 1945. (*Van Dijk family archive*)

*Left*: The marriage of Bonno van Dijken and Clasien de Jong, 12 June 1944. (*Van Dijken family archive*)

# Chapter 5

# The Aftermath

After the execution in Zwolle there were two more reprisals where men were taken out of the *Huis van Bewaring*. Besides the previously mentioned execution at the Geldersedijk in Hattem, where six men were shot, there was also an execution on 10 April. At the Katerveer in Zwolle nine men were shot. One man escaped execution by dropping into the water at the last moment.[1]

On 5 May 1945 the Second World War officially ended in the Netherlands. Zwolle had already been liberated on the night of 13/14 April by the Canadian Leo Major. The reconstruction of the Netherlands started and those that were suspected of various crimes needed to be judged. While the victors made plans to prevent a new world war and to deal with crimes on a national scale, there were also local initiatives to give the countless personal tragedies of those five years a place.

Only after Zwolle had been liberated, did it become obvious what happened that fatal morning of 31 March 1945. Women had lost their husbands and children were left fatherless. The Second World War had left its destructive traces in these families and all of them dealt with it differently. Part of the peace they found came from the trials of the Germans and their collaborators. In the last months of the war various atrocities had been committed for which they were held accountable. Still, some managed to get off lighter than others.

In the case of the execution at the Meppelerstraatweg, the Germans and their superiors involved, had a lot of infighting. Further confusion was caused by the different reasons people gave for the retaliation or lies that were told. They mentioned an attack on the railway between Zwolle-Meppel, but also an attack on a Red Cross train by underground organizations.[2]

# TRAGEDY AND BETRAYAL IN THE DUTCH RESISTANCE

## Hendrica van Dijk

After she had been liberated by the Canadians in the north, Hendrica was sent home with cigarettes for her husband. However, she would never be able to give them to him, as he had been shot without her knowledge. Hendrica later married Egbertus Manders, with whom she would have no children. The marriage wasn't happy and only after her second husband died in 1960 did her life become better. However, tragedy further struck the family when two of her children died young. Jan died in a motor accident in 1961, while Piet died due to kidney disease in 1966.[3]

Hendrica van Dijk was left to raise the children, ca. 1947. (*Van Dijk family archive*)

## THE AFTERMATH

Aeldert Sattler helped her after the war by getting an allowance and wrote a letter to Stichting '40-'45. He refused to talk with journalists that wanted to write a book about the underground in Zwolle, as he suspected that during a potential Russian invasion the illegal groups would come become active again.

Hendrica had plans to move back to Noord-Brabant, where her family lived. She could be with them again and could find some support for her family, however, she stayed in Zwolle. The family, including the children, struggled with their difficulties. There was material damage, as well as mental scars. The two oldest children were sent to an orphan school, that also accepted half-orphans and there they learned a profession. Hendrica worked at the school as a cook, while taking care of her daughter. The youngest child was looked after by her in-laws. Those were busy days for Hendrica. She got up early to get her house in order and went to school with her daughter returning around 4.30pm.[4]

The family also received thanks from the American government for their help to Allied airmen. This was a certificate stamped with Dwight D. Eisenhower's autograph, the Supreme Allied Commander. This certificate was handed out 4,870 times and sent to people who had helped between one and eight aircrew members.[5]

Gerrit van Dijk, the brother of Wilhelmus, continued a military career and became commander of the outdoor security in various internment camps. NSB-members, suspected traitors, Dutch collaborators and Germans were kept in there. At these camps he also met his new wife, who worked there as a secretary. After the camps were finished, he took up his old profession with the tannery. He died in 1972. Piet, the son of Gerrit, was called up to serve with the marines and later held various professions.[6]

After the war, Piet van Dijk, the brother of Wilhelmus, took care of Wilhelmus's grave, where his parents were later buried. Regularly he went with his children to the grave and painted the letters inscribed on the stone. He also ensured that Wilhelmus and Hendrica were granted the Resistance Memorial Cross. Piet died in 1987.

Hendrica died on 4 December 1991. Her daughter Joke died in 2008. Wilhelmus van Dijk had been buried at the Catholic cemetery in Zwolle, but was reburied on what would be his 110th birthday at the Nationaal Ereveld Loenen, a cemetery of honour, together with his parents.

## Gerharda Bosch

While she had heard rumours, Gerharda was uncertain about the fate of her husband. Only on 14 April did a preacher tell her that Hermanus Bosch had been shot at the Meppelerstraatweg. On 25 April Hermanus was buried and the coffin was covered in flowers. There was a flower arrangement from the KP Friesland, the group based in the region Friesland, and a wreath from the Dutch Interior Forces, fighting component, 2nd company. The local preachers Munnik and Thijs presided at the funeral.

After the war Gerharda moved to the Hemerkerstraat in Zwolle. From her living room she could see the monument that was dedicated to her dead husband, a painful reminder of her loss. She requested to have the monument moved, which was put in the place where it currently stands. She died in 1967. Hermanus and Gerharda are buried at the cemetery Kranenburg in Zwolle.[7]

Hermanus Bosch with his parents, wife and son Herman, ca. 1945. (*Bosch family archive*)

# THE AFTERMATH

Hermanus Bosch wasn't just missed by his family, but also his friends from the underground organizations. Piet van den Berg, who had been in contact with him, wrote the following eulogy:

> The Resistance in Overijssel started in and around its large population centres: Twente and Zwolle. The last city in particular with its conscious national bourgeoisie was slowly, but surely on the rise. It was no wonder, therefore, that long before September 1944, Herman Bosch's house was already a focal point for the Resistance. Coupons and illegal reading material were 'processed', people in hiding were picked up and taken away: even prisoners from Amersfoort [concentration camp] who were transported through Zwolle were successfully liberated and then cared for.
>
> In a few words the work of a Dutchman has been drawn here, who, with the commitment of himself and his family, has done everything, that his hand found to do and what lay in his power. He also worked through the 'Mad Tuesday', despite many difficulties and personal disappointments. His house was always open to his illegal friends: no risk was too much for his wife. Unfortunately, he also had to fall for the Liberation of his country, without being allowed to experience that Liberation. All of us reading this will only be able to honour him and his other friends by working day and night with the same selflessness and fatherly love for a better future. In this way we know how to act in Herman's spirit. He met death in a brave way. I hope that later Herman and his friends will not only be commemorated because of their attitude at a time when we, as a people, were having a hard time, but I hope that his son can later say: My father has fallen at work, that was completed by his friends. In our commemoration we will have to try to retain the spiritual gains from the war and occupation. Then commemoration brings duty to reflection. A reflection that will lead to the flourishing of our country and people.[8]

Why Hermanus was arrested is unknown. After the war the courier Trijntje Kamphuis, who was nicknamed 'Diesel', said that treason had been involved, but she couldn't talk about it. Her nerves had taken too much and she had to be admitted to an institution.[9]

## Willemien Sebel

The body of Willem Sebel was transported to Lutten in a cargo bike by his brother-in-law Bertus and a friend from the Resistance Huub van der Kamp. They made the trip of 40 kilometres to bring his remains home. The night before his wife Willemien had been informed and on 5 April 1945 Willem Sebel was buried in Lutten. The death of Sebel shook the local community.[10]

Willemien was left behind to take care of the children. She remodelled her husband's overcoat into a winter coat. Every year on 4 May (the *Dodenherdenking*) when the people of the Netherlands remember in two minutes silence those who fell in the Second World War, Willemien felt weak. She died in 2002.[11]

The Sebel family was also left without a father, 1946. (*Sebel family archive*)

Willem Sebel was posthumously awarded the Eisenhower certificate, because he had helped to transport the Allied pilots. He was also granted the Resistance Memorial Cross. His grave is still in Lutten.[12]

## Gerritdina IJzerman

On 31 March Gerritdina IJzerman heard rumours about the death of her husband. She refused to believe this, trusting Martens' promise that he would try to prevent the capital punishment. When she went to Zwolle on 6 April, she didn't receive much more information. There she met Martens, but he couldn't tell her much news. People had indeed been executed, but he hoped that Jan Muller and Berend IJzerman weren't among them. In reality he had known they were shot but didn't want to tell Gerritdina.

She wanted answers and went to an undertaker, who told her that Berend and four others had been shot on 31 March. Her family had known this, but no one knew how to explain it to her.

On the day that Berend's passing became known, his daughter Emmy was playing outside. Other children approached her and said: 'Your father is dead.' She got so upset that she took off her clogs and hit the children with them. Only when she came home did she find out the children had been right.

On 12 April 1945 Berend Jan IJzerman was buried in Kampen. A while after the funeral an elder stopped at the IJzerman residence. He told her that the death of her husband had been a punishment from God. The elder was immediately shown the door and afterwards the family refused to have anything to do with the church.

The family had a tough time as they received little support. The life insurance wasn't paid out because it had been a violent death. The enamel factory also offered little support, but the baker Broekhorst and a local butcher gave them leftovers. Later the organization Stichting '40-'45 offered help. In the evenings Gerritdina repaired her children's clothes. She had been weakened by the whole ordeal. The stress of the war had also weakened her heart. An operation and medication made little difference and she died in 1979.[13]

Rumours that Berend IJzerman had been shot at the Veerallee in Zwolle because he had taken pictures of German positions were not true. This story contains some truth, but it has been changed by retellings.[14]

# TRAGEDY AND BETRAYAL IN THE DUTCH RESISTANCE

Berend Jan IJzerman is buried at the cemetery De Zandbergen in IJsselmuiden, a few rows from the grave of Jan Muller. After her death Gerritdina was cremated and her ashes were placed in her husband's grave. The Resistance Memorial Cross was also granted to Berend Jan IJzerman.[15]

## Maria Muller

Maria Muller came back physically weakened from Westerbork. The journey had left her exhausted and it was only when she had returned home that she discovered that her husband had been shot. She never fully recovered, had little contact with other people and was nervous. She remained a vulnerable lady and for the rest of her life she mourned the loss of her beloved husband. She died in 1967.

Bep, the daughter of Jan and Maria, lived in Kampen with her mother for a while and got a job at the Stichting '40-'45 in Kampen. She died in 2009. Throughout her life, she looked for a place to tell her father's story.[16]

Joop, the son of Jan and Maria, watched the funeral from a distance, hiding behind a tree. After the Second World War Joop went as a

The burial of Jan Muller, 1945. (*Muller family archive*)

volunteer with the Dutch army to the Dutch East Indies and served there for three years. He spoke little about his experiences, but suffered from stress and nightmares. When he was 42, he had a heart attack. He held a grudge against the Germans, and loved it when his son received unsatisfactory grades for the German language. He refused to eat eels for the rest of his life, due to the one that came out of the corpse's nose. He died in 1993.[17]

Jan Muller is buried together with his wife, daughter and son-in-law at the cemetery De Zandbergen in IJsselmuiden. A few rows behind him rests Berend Jan IJzerman with his wife.

## Hendrika Langkamp

Hendrika, the wife of Johan Langkamp, stayed in prison until she was liberated by the Canadians. After she was freed, she discovered that her husband had been shot. Later the clothes that her husband had worn at the execution were brought to her house. In the back of the neck on one garment there was a small bullet hole. A few months later her mother died. She never remarried and spoke little about her deceased husband to her three children. She died in 2006.[18]

Johan Langkamp received the Resistance Memorial Cross and the Mobilisation War Cross. Johan Langkamp is buried at the cemetery Kranenburg in Zwolle. When Hendrika died she was placed in the same grave.

## Thijs Brouwer

Thijs Brouwer, who was locked up together with Wilhelmus van Dijk, was interviewed by the Germans on Monday, 9 April 1945. Cieraad, the collaborator, was present to serve as a translator. Brouwer was questioned about how he knew Wilhelmus van Dijk. Brouwer replied that Wilhelmus had offered to repair his bike and that they worked together before that at the shipping company Koppe. Cieraad confirmed this, because he had been present at the arrest. After being told that Wilhelmus van Dijk had been executed, Brouwer was released. He died in 1978.[19]

## Bonno van Dijken

Bonno van Dijken had been a part of 'De Groene' and had attacked the railway tracks several times, including the failed attack on the railway bridge to the south of Zwolle. He married Clasien de Jong, who had also been involved with the illegal activities of her husband. When the Allies liberated Zwolle, a strange situation occurred. The Interior Forces were needed again, but this time to protect the collaborators and members of the NSB from the wrath of the people. The tables had suddenly turned and the former enemies were now people that needed to be protected. Still, Bonno despised the fact that the people who hadn't done anything against the Germans, suddenly wanted their revenge. Bonno van Dijken stayed close with his friends from the underground organizations, even regularly visiting one that had to spend time in prison, and he attended the memorial service at the monument at the Meppelerstraatweg. A leftover from the war, was that Bonno hated cows for the rest of his life, due to them following him across the pastures on the nightly raids. Bonno died in 2009. Clasien passed away in 2015.[20]

## Gerhardus Alferink

When Gerhardus Alferink was arrested, together with Willem Sebel, he still had 70,000. guilders at home. This was meant to help people in hiding and Alferink was supposed to bring it to the suburbs that were too far for the couriers. His wife brought the money to another address, where Mr Verheul would take care of it and continue distributing it. Alferink was transferred to a punishment school in Zwolle, but because he reported sick, he was released on 11 April 1945.

On 16 April 1945, after Zwolle had been liberated, he saw Nico Polderman, who had handed over the notes from Willem Sebel and Johan Langkamp to the Germans, standing on the corner of the Assendorperstraat-Bartjensstraat with a Sten gun. Alferink asked him: 'What's happening here?' Polderman replied: 'As you can see, I'm with the Interior Forces.' Alferink got in touch with the police to have Polderman arrested, but it didn't happen. Alferink died in 1968.[21]

# THE AFTERMATH

## Richard Fuller

Richard Fuller, the American who had been at Wilhelmus's house, stayed for two weeks at his new address, the Hertenstraat 38 in Zwolle, and from there went to Vilsteren. He was in the possession of forged identity papers, which stated that his name was Johan de Wit, a contractor from Wisch. His journey to freedom later went through Heino and ended in Zelham where Fuller was liberated by the advancing Allies on 1 April 1945. For 116 days he managed to evade the Germans. He died in 2012.[22]

## Eyewitnesses

The execution made an impact on the lives of those that had seen it. Casperus Tardi was so upset by the whole ordeal that he had to go home. Harm-Jan Otterman and his son Wim agreed to never speak about it again. Only fifty years later Wim started talking about it.[23] Johannes Jansen continued to Meppel with the 'hungerfarers'. Once home he told his family about the horrific act he had seen. He died in 1974.[24] It was said that, Heimert Oordijk, shortly after the execution, placed a simple cross consisting of two wooden slats at the place where the men were shot. Heimert Oordijk died in 1947. It is unknown whether the war influenced his premature death.[25]

# Chapter 6

# Perpetrators and Collaborators

Now that the war was over and the fighting ceased, the German perpetrators and their collaborators needed to be held responsible for their actions. Several of those involved were captured, but not all of them were found. Those that were caught would have to justify their acts and face the consequences of their actions.

## Piet Richard Cieraad

Cieraad, nicknamed 'the Butcher of Zwolle', who was once so proud of his busy nights 'with finishing off' illegal workers, was mistreated after his arrest by people involved in former underground organisations. As a result, his cheekbone was broken. While he was in prison, his mother wrote various letters, even to the Dutch queen to plead for her son. She left out the parts where her son was responsible for many deaths. Cieraad decided to renounce his Nazi-beliefs and co-operated with his questioners. However, what he told involved a lot of lies to make himself appear better. In his trial the death penalty was demanded, but this was changed to life imprisonment in 1947.

In his cell Cieraad repented and became a practising Christian. In 1957 his life-long prison sentence was changed to a temporary one, aided by Cieraad's wife and Pastor Keers. The church saw itself as the guardian of the family and wanted to help in Cieraad's case. Factors that influenced the decision for the changed sentence was Cieraad's difficult youth, his German wife, the lack of guidance from his father and his young age. In the autumn of 1958 Cieraad was released and he pretended exemplary behaviour.

In reality he terrorized his family and hadn't abandoned his Nazi-beliefs. In 1963 he wished to get back his right to vote, which expired during his trial. Cieraad was insulted and felt as if he was treated as a second-class citizen because he couldn't vote. While the church celebrated the repentance and release of Cieraad as a success, for his family it was a disaster. He died in 2004 in Naarden.¹

## Jacob Lijs

Near the end of March 1945, a warning was issued by the underground organisations in Kampen. It was printed in the illegal press 'Strijdend Nederland':

> 'Urgent warning! [...] The common Resistance groups warn the population of Kampen with the most urgency of every acquaintance, every relation, or every contact with the following people, who all directly or indirectly are engaged in traitor's work for the German SD. [...]
>
> Jacques Lijs, lives Burgwal 54. Is a very dangerous SD-agent and works in Kampen under his own name as a provoker. He also has various cover names such as Van Loon. Around 45-years-old, normal height, Indonesian type, sometimes wears glasses without rims; has a somewhat weird look in his eyes; is hypnotiser, homosexual and morphinist. Lijs has contact with the son of Mr Lucas from the music store Goldschmeiding [...]
>
> Curb your curiosity. Remember that a loose word can have irredeemable consequences. Remain silent even against your family and friends. As soon as you have released something, you've lost control over it. You don't know where it goes. Watch out! Keep your eyes and ears open. Report us every activity and investigate. Report their names, without mentioning the source from which your information has been derived, and in this manner assure that the henchmen of the enemy are the centre of attention. In such a way we paralyse their activity. Pass on this publication only to your utmost reliable acquaintances. With your caution and silence you aid our fight.
>
> The common Resistance groups.'²

For Berend IJzerman and Jan Muller the warning came too late, because they had already been captured on 26 February by the SD. However, the warning made it impossible for Lijs to remain in Kampen the last few weeks of the war and, after wandering around for some time, he ended up in Belgium. It became difficult to acquire morphine and he heard voices in his head. He reported to a sanatorium, where he could easily mingle among the patients there. Eventually he was arrested by the political investigation service. 'I've gambled and lost,' Lijs said after his arrest. He was interned in Wezep.

Lijs explained his behaviour and his reports on the underground in Kampen as follows:

> These reports were largely confusing the truth and misguiding. I did this to get more morphine from [*the SD*]. He gave me only once morphine. He did give me smoking articles and once liquor. I inflated my expense account to buy morphine on the black market.[3]

Albert Gort, who had helped Lijs, denied any involvement in Lijs's activities. He explained his meetings with the Germans at the Vloeddijk in Kampen as friendly visits, as he did more often. Despite this the two were often seen together.[4]

During the trial the following report was made:

> ***Psychiatric report of Jacob Lijs, conducted by Mr E. van Schothorst on May 9, 1947:***
> History as told by the suspect himself: Since the suspect is seriously disturbed, simulated or not, it is hard to record a history with him. According to his own data as a child he never had any symptoms of nervous or neurotic predisposition. He went to primary school, but twice he didn't advance to the next year. Afterwards he graduated from the MULO and received a third-year diploma. Afterwards he studied for a state exam and he got a job as an inspector of the ENIS mortgage bank in [the Dutch East Indies]. In this job he earned a lot of money, so that to invest his money he took over an orchid plantation, a woman's fashion store and a pharmacy.

## PERPETRATORS AND COLLABORATORS

While in [the Dutch East Indies] he got a liver disease that gave him a lot of pain. For this he was injected with morphine by the treating doctor. This morphine gave him a complete anaesthesia, but also a wonderful feeling of well-being. Initially he left it at the injections, but gradually he became addicted to morphine and started injecting morphine himself, morphine which he initially got on prescriptions from a doctor and later by supplying himself in all sorts of illegal ways.

He then declined to such an extent that he said he had forgotten to extend his residence permit in Indies. As a result, he was deported from [the Dutch East Indies]. He then went to Nice and later to Monte Carlo. The morphine use continued, so he gradually got rid of all his money. Afterwards he went to his mother in The Hague, where he settled.

Later, after being admitted to various institutions to be nursed and helped to get rid of his morphine use (among others, in Woensel, Vught, the Ramaerkliniek, Endegeest and Willem Arntz Foundation in Utrecht), he went to Kampen. A temporary improvement always occurred, at least he was released because he behaved completely correctly in the institution and in this way led the doctors to attempt probation with him. His last admission to the crimes was in the Willem Arntz Foundation in Utrecht, where he stayed from 16 August to 26 November 1944. On 26-11-1944 he was then released from the Willem Arntz Foundation on probationary leave. He then went back to Kampen, where the various offences, for which he must now stand, took place.

Since I am very keen to get more information about his history, I got in touch with his brother [...] in Kampen. Said gentleman told me that the delinquent, who is ten years younger than him, was already behaving badly as a young child. He was spoiled and pampered by his mother, while his father and [brother] from Kampen, always tried to get him on the right track. At the age of 8 it became clear that delinquent was absolutely untrustworthy. He stole money several times and was also crooked in other areas. Moreover, he fantasized strongly. When delinquent was around 16 years old, his mother went to see a miracle doctor. This happened because the mother had certain complaints. However, the miracle doctor was much more interested in the delinquent, to whom he felt attracted and decided to appoint him as an assistant.

He then worked for about a year with this miracle doctor and at the age of 18 delinquent started his own practice in the profession of miracle doctor. He held office hours in Kampen and the surrounding area. The money flowed in excessively, yet delinquent was always destitute, as a result of which the brother afterwards came to the conclusion, that it is quite possible that the delinquent had already come into contact with morphine at the time. The family has had a lot of concerns about the delinquent. The reason why he had left the Indies was, according to the brother, due to the fact that he had managed to get the natives under his influence and that he wanted to found a conchi [*free state*] in Indonesia to help the natives to gain independence.[5] Because of this he was dangerous to the state and he was removed from the Indies.

In later years, the delinquent began to practise magnetism and spiritualism. The brother once experienced a seance and although he does not believe in spiritualism, he has experienced the most wonderful and incomprehensible things. The brother considered the delinquent very dangerous and completely unreliable. According to him, the person investigated was also well known to the vice police in The Hague. Even at the time he was working on magnetism and spiritualism, the delinquent was always accompanied by the most exceptional male types so that according to the brother there was at least reason to think of homosexuality.

Family history: The father of the examined has been a perfectly normal person, who was sometimes angry, but who in no way could be called abnormal. At a later age, the man started to suffer from sugar disease and he died of pneumonia. The mother is also a perfectly normal woman, who can be called very strong both physically and mentally. The fact that she has been treated by a miracle doctor, naturally gives some thought. No cases of mental illness occurred in the further family. The brother in Kampen is also a completely normal, very progressive man.

Research: In my research, I was able to establish that the delinquent can currently be considered completely abnormal. He suffers severely from hearing and, as he says himself, feeling hallucinations. He believes that there's a plot against him and that the members of this conspiracy are the ones who, by constantly telling him ambiguous sentences, typing on his writing machine and all kinds of other hallucinations, want to keep him from the right track.

He is quite tactless. The whole, however, gives me the impression of at least a [thickening] and even partly simulating. The psychopath is noticeable in him. He is flattering and theatrical. There are no doubt hysterical moments. His motor skills are also very active. Furthermore, it appears that he has a strong selfish attitude and that he actually finds himself a very good person, because he confessed his sins before God. He thinks it is a scandal that the conspiracy against him treats him in this way. A normal conversation cannot be sustained with the examined because he is always distracted by his hearing hallucinations. He has a great loss of decorum and is severely degenerated. He sheds tears of laughter at the most silly things; completely unrestrained. He misses the little finger of his left hand. Asked about this, he tells that he severed it while sculpting. His brother in Kampen asked about this, however, declares that the delinquent has chopped off his little finger in order to get money. Throughout the research I get the strong impression of simulating. I got to know him as a completely unreliable person with a very bad character. He is, in particular, someone who is capable of anything and not only because of morphinomania, but also because of his psychopathy. He can therefore be regarded as completely criminal.

Diagnosis: A criminal psychopath with morphinomania.

Conclusion: From everything I have heard I can come to the conclusion that we are dealing here with a constitutional psychopath, and moreover there are undoubtedly hysterical moments. The start of the morphinomania could be the contact with the miracle doctor, or the injections he received for his liver disease in the Indies. The fact that he is a psychopath with hysterical traits is the cause that the person investigated has completely surrendered to morphine. […]

Regarding the questions asked by the police commissioner, Mr Lettinck, I come to the following answers in my conclusion. 1st: No doubt, while committing the charges as laid out against him, he was suspected of having suffered abnormal development and ailing malfunctioning of his mental capacities, in particular psychopathy and morphinomania. 2nd: This abnormal development and ailing malfunctioning have without doubt at least limited his ability to acknowledge the scope and the unauthorized of the committed facts, while they were also the cause that [the person] examined could not determine his own will. 3rd: It can be assumed that the facts committed were not outside the influence of the abovementioned abnormal developments and ailing malfunctioning of his mental capacities.

Advice: It is obvious that this man is very dangerous for society, that repetition of similar facts is actually certain and if not similar, then other very serious facts. It is therefore necessary for this man to be removed from social society for some time. However, given that we are not dealing with a normal person here, I cannot recommend imprisonment, but I think it is perfectly justified to have this man eligible for long-term internment in a government working institution.[6]

Jacob Lijs was never sentenced for his crimes, because on 24 July 1947 he was found dead in prison. The section report gave: 'bleeding due to injury caused by Lijs himself' as cause of death.[7]

## Nicolaas Polderman

After the execution of Willem Sebel, on 31 March 1945, and Johan Langkamp, on 29 March 1945, Polderman dared to ask his fellow prisoners about the notes that he had handed over to the Germans. When a fellow prisoner didn't trust him, Polderman asked if he thought he was helping the SD.

When Zwolle was liberated, the prisoners were released from their cells. Polderman was one of them, being released by the Dutch Interior Forces and he joined that organisation. Thereupon he received an armband and a machine pistol. As a member of the Interior Forces he carried out various assignments.[8]

When a certain suspect needed to be arrested, Polderman stood guard outside to prevent any escape. The rest of the arresting team would go inside. When the suspect had been taken out of the gutter, he made a peculiar move and a member of the Interior Forces fired a warning shot. Thereupon Polderman stormed inside, up the stairs and fired while still on the hallway of the first floor upwards into the room where the arrested man was present. That suspect got a bullet through his leg but if the Sten gun had been set to automatic, he would have lost his entire foot.

After the wounded man was taken care off, he was brought to the *Huis van Bewaring*. There Polderman stood outside, while Hendrik Spijkerman, who was working there, saw him. When Spijkerman was talking with the leader of the arresting team, Polderman put his gun against a wall and ran away. Other attempts, among others by Spijkerman, to detain Polderman, failed. When it became too dangerous in Zwolle, Polderman moved to Ede. Here he was eventually captured and incarcerated. On 22 July 1947 he escaped from the auxiliary prison at the Kanaalweg in Rotterdam, but was quickly recaptured.

According to a report Polderman didn't understand the consequences of his actions. He pretended to be a bigger person than he truly was and he had no insight into what his actions caused.

On 31 January 1949 Polderman was sentenced to three years in prison, without deduction of custody, for 'willfully during the time of the current war […] aiding the enemy'. From all other charges he was cleared. He became known as a weakling that couldn't resist temptations, acted without thinking with tendencies to criminality and vagrancy.[9]

During his time in prison, Polderman wished to work in the mines in Limburg, although there was objection to this from Zwolle. He was released eventually. In 1951 he married a woman ten years older but the marriage ended in 1965. He remarried in 1966, this time to a woman twelve years younger. He had four children. Nicolaas Polderman died on 1 January 1979 in Hopfgarten im Brixem, Austria.[10]

## Hans Kolitz

Hans Kolitz was sentenced by the *Bijzonder Gerechtshof Arnhem,* (Special Court of Justice Arnhem) to five years in prison for his involvement in putting together the lists of *Todeskandidaten.* These were forwarded by him and he recommended in Deventer and Zwolle the execution of suspects of severe crimes. For his defence Kolitz explained:

> If at the time my confessions have been recorded by the police as facts, which I currently deny, this is entirely the result of the fact that back then I understood almost no Dutch and during the interrogations there was no translator present. I have explicitly pointed out to the police officials that at that time I already suspected that what they wrote down in Dutch was not according to my statement.
> 
> After the surrender I got the impression from Schöngarth that he wanted to shrug off his responsibility to me. I can explain this because during my imprisonment – I think in September 1945 – I heard from Major Laber that Schöngarth had committed fraud during the surrender to the army of the Canadians. A list was supposed to be made up of the troop detachments that had surrendered; as *obersturmbannführer* I was at the top of the list regarding my detachment, while behind my name stood 'head department IV'. According to Laber, Schöngarth

supposedly ordered an hour before the official surrender that the page whereupon I was marked had to be ripped out and an order was given to an *oberleutenant*, whose name I do not recall, to insert a new page instead, whereupon he, by the orders of Schöngarth, had to write that I was a replacement [*Befehlshaber der Sicherheitsdienst*] [...] In this regard I would like to remark that the interrogation conducted at that time was not in such a calm manner as currently, while I must assume that people then due to lack of knowledge of business did not understand how the case was put together. Furthermore, I understood little Dutch and the reporters understood little German. Also, there was no translator present.

While I knew that my statements, as they were recorded, were not correctly reproduced, which I also told the reporters, I ultimately still signed. I went along with this, because we would be shot according to messages, so that it mattered little what was recorded.

It was also admitted by the inspector of the police that the police report was closed some six months after the hearings had taken place. The months March and April 1945 were the worst of his life according to Kolitz.[11]

To give a broader scope of Kolitz's acts, the following story must also be told. Anton Schrader was arrested by the Germans and locked up:

> Concerning my abuse I can remember that Kolitz during a meeting asked what was wrong with my ear. I pressed a hand against it due to the pain in my ear, whereupon I said that I was beaten there. To what degree he took measures I do not know, but the next day someone treated my ear. At that time I didn't tell Kolitz that I had been beaten with a stick, while I did tell it to [Joseph] Schreieder.

During the rapid Allied advance, Kolitz had also suggested to the SD in Zwolle and Deventer that prisoners that were suspected of serious offences, should be shot. Kolitz eventually was removed from Dutch territory on 16 February 1951.[12]

## Hanns Albin Rauter

*Höhere SS- und Polizeiführer* Rauter was sentenced by the *Bijzonder Gerechtshof Den Haag* to death for carrying out a terror regime in the Netherlands. Among others his involvement in the persecution of Jews, and the acts of terror against the civilian population justified this sentence. The process started on 1 April 1948 and Rauter was executed on 25 March 1949 on the Waalsdorpervlakte.[13]

## Karl Schöngarth

From 7 March 1945 onwards *Befehlshaber der Sicherheitspolizei und des SD* Karl Schöngarth served as a replacement for Rauter, who had been wounded during the attack at the Woeste Hoeve. He was nearly cleared of charges by a British court due to a lack of evidence. Schöngarth was involved in the Galle-case in Enschede, where he had the American airman Americo S. Galle executed who was dressed in civilian clothes. He was sentenced to hanging in February 1946 and on 16 May 1946 the punishment was carried out.[14]

## Joseph Rauch

The former head of the SD in Zwolle was handed over to Yugoslavia after the war. From 1941 to 1944 he had worked there as part of the *Geheime Feldpolizei*. Whether he ever was sentenced is unclear. He died in prison on 9 October 1949.[15]

## Walter Bartels

Walter Bartels, Rauch's subordinate, was detained in the Netherlands and questioned by the police about his activities with the SD. The wife of Bartels wrote letters to the Dutch queen to ask for the release of her husband. He had always behaved humanely. Her eight-year-old daughter prayed at church for the return of her father and asked her questions: 'Mother, we pray every night for our father to come home. Why hasn't he returned? Doesn't the dear God hear us?' Bartels' wife didn't know what to answer to this. She also didn't know about her husband beating two prisoners on the head with an iron ruler. His home in Germany was bombed. Bartels received no punishment as on 12 August 1949 it was decided there were more urgent cases. Bartels was transported from the Netherlands to Germany on 15 September 1949.[16]

## Fritz Winter

Fritz Winter, who had led the execution at the Meppelerstraatweg, was detained on 8 July 1947 in a German internment camp. In Brussels, where he had worked previously, there was a trial against him and on 5 February 1949 he was transferred to the Netherlands for judging. Winter was sentenced by the *Bijzonder Gerechtshof Arnhem* first to two years in prison. His time in arrest influenced the sentence. Winter had the sentence appealed and got six months in prison. It wasn't shown that Winter had wilfully operated against the regulations. He assumed that those executed on the Meppelerstraatweg had been sentenced to death and didn't doubt the lawfulness of this conviction. Winter made a comparison between the police actions in Indonesia and his position. Were soldiers in a position to ignore orders? The answer was no, which helped Winter to reduce his sentence. On 17 January 1950 he was transported to Germany.[17]

## Friedrich Genczyk

Friedrich Genczyk, who had been present at the execution on the Meppelerstraatweg, was sentenced by the *Bijzonder Gerechtshof Arnhem* first to two and a half years in prison, but this was appealed to two years, with deduction of his arrest, for his complicity in a war crime. His was wife sick and he himself was aged. On 1 March 1950 he was moved to Germany.[18]

## Reinhard Stuck

Stuck, who had stopped the traffic at the Meppelerstraatweg, was arrested and transferred to the Netherlands. While he was in detention, a letter came on 31 May 1948, written by the *Sozialdemokratische Partei Deutschlands,* the Social Democratic Party of Germany:

> Reinhard Stuck was already before 1933 a member of the SPD and not only a member, but also an exceptionally active employee in our ranks. Through this he attracted the hostility of the national socialists, so that he [shortly] after the 'Machtergreifung' [*seizure of power*], was removed from the service and on the ground of Paragr. 4 from the 'Beamtensauberungsgezetz' [*official cleansing law*] excluded from the educational service. For him it was no longer possible to practice his profession and he was forced to sustain himself as an agent for a life insurance company. This activity was halted in 1939 when he was called up to serve in the army. [This] wasn't on the ground of any military training, but he was called up to serve as a simple soldier.

Stuck was released on 25 November 1948 from camp Vught and moved to Germany.[19]

## Rudolf Schmidt

Rudolf Schmidt, who was present at the execution at the Meppelerstraatweg, was released on 27 April 1946, but his freedom didn't last long. He was arrested again on 17 September 1946. On 20 October 1948 it was decided that he would not be prosecuted and on 25 November he was released from camp Vught and transported to Germany.[20]

## Wilhelm Hukriede

Wilhelm Hukriede, who had also stopped traffic during the execution, was held in a German camp, where Fritz Winter was also present. Here he received interesting information, which he explained:

> When I was in camp Fischbeck with Dr Winter he repeatedly told me: 'If only I knew for which case people

want to bring me to the Netherlands, then I could prepare myself for it.' I asked him if he had done so much wrong, because he had been quite nervous.

[He] told me repeatedly that he had been present with [executions] at the Ijssel and the Meppelerstraatweg in Zwolle, in Apeldoorn and in Almelo. He said that [during the execution at Katerveer] he only blocked the road, but that he'd rather not think about this execution. He did not want to go into details about this execution.

In September 1948 the court decided that there would be no charges against Hukriede. He was released from camp Vught on 26 October and transported to Germany, where he was in time to celebrate Christmas with his family.[21]

## Fritz Martens

Fritz Martens, who oversaw the case against Jan Muller and Berend IJzerman, was captured in the Netherlands and stayed here until his release. In 1947 he was in camp Avegoor, but on 5 November 1947 transferred to camp Vught. He was released from camp Vught on 8 September 1948. His wife and children had to leave behind everything when they fled from the Red Army.[22]

## Willy Mönnich

Willy Mönnich, who had helped Bartels during his investigations, was captured and tried in the Netherlands. When he was in prison, his wife wrote from Germany about two cases that pleaded for her husband. In one of those cases Mönnich had prevented a Jewish woman Sonja Grams, who was married to a German, being sent to the concentration camp Theresienstadt. The man was also released from a concentration camp with the help of Mönnich, because the procedure had been followed incorrectly. On 17 December 1948 it was decided that Mönnich could be released. He returned home to his wife and children.[23]

## Erich Hohmann

Erich Hohmann, whose pistol had malfunctioned during the execution, was transported to the Netherlands on 18 November 1947. A court decided that there would be no charges pressed against him. On 26 October 1948 he was transported to Germany.[24]

## The *Huis van Bewaring* in Zwolle

The *Huis van Bewaring* was directly used after the war by the Dutch authorities to lock up suspected persons. However, this time, the suspects were members of the NSB and people that were suspected of German sympathies. Until 2004 it was used to detain people. The building was sold in 2005 and opened again in 2008. Currently it houses the Librije Hotel and restaurant De Librije. One of the old cells is kept intact to give an impression of the history of the building.

# Chapter 7

# The Monument and Reflections

The Cambridge dictionary defines a monument as follows: 'a structure or building that is built to honour a special person or event'. They also give an example: 'In the square in front of the hotel stands a monument to all the people killed in the war.'[1] In other words, monuments are placed to remember a specific moment in the past and serve as anchors in the present to past events. However, these monuments also pass through time, as at different moments they can mean different things and also the knowledge that they must pass on is different.

Throughout the Netherlands there are monuments dedicated to the Second World War. These can range from plaquettes on a wall, to stained glass windows, to concrete structures. They remember certain groups, such as residents from a village that died, or are dedicated to specific events, such as shot-down airplanes. One of those monuments stands at the Meppelerstraatweg, dedicated to the tragic shooting on 31 March 1945 and a reflection on this gives some insight into how this event has been treated in history.

In the past, shortly after the execution happened, a wooden cross was placed at the Meppelerstraatweg. It indicated to people of Zwolle and those that came by that something had happened there. The markings were simple, as most people that came across it must have been vaguely aware of what it stood for.

Later a more solid monument was erected to remember the five men. A wooden cross wasn't durable enough. This monument consisted of a brick wall, which indicated that people died on that location, but didn't mention their names: 'Glory to those that fell here for us. Zwolle 31 March 1945. On this sad spot there fell five men by Hitler's roguish servants. They died for us all.'[2] It was quite nationalistic in appearance.

# TRAGEDY AND BETRAYAL IN THE DUTCH RESISTANCE

In 1960 a total of 5,480 guilders was paid by the government for a new monument. Three stonemasons responded to the contract, although one of them was rejected, because the family hadn't behaved properly during the Second World War.[3] Around the same time two little vandals, Jan and Herman, both seven years old, destroyed the old monument. Their parents were informed by the police.[4]

In 1963 the new monument was revealed. It still stands on a green area between two roads, with two flag poles next to it. A stone cross on a plateau with five sawn-off trees, symbolizing the cut-short lives of the men, reminds passerbys of what happened there on that fatal morning 31 March 1945. It was not regarded with national pride, but seen as a tragedy.

The monument consists of a stone plateau, whereupon five pillars are placed. These pillars are cut-off, symbolizing the lives of the men that were cut short on that fatal morning. A cross next to it, reminds the people of those that died. An inscription shows the names of the five men, when they were born and where. Two flagpoles stand next to the monument, one with the Dutch flag, the other with the flag from Zwolle. The monument is not at the place of the execution itself, but a few metres from it. The wording also makes it clear why the monument is there:

>Gefusilleerd 31 maart 1945 (*shot 31 March 1945*)
>H. Bosch           * 5 - 1 – 1914 te Kampen
>W. A. van Dijk     * 10 - 11 – 1908 te Zwolle
>J. A. Muller       * 24 - 5 - 1890 te Rotterdam
>W. Sebel           * 4 - 4 – 1901 te Vlaardingen
>B. J. IJzerman     * 14 - 1 – 1911 te Kampen

The choice to add text, or to leave it out, is a conscious decision and has implications to the present. In the case of the first solid monument, the brick wall with the plaquette, it was obvious to people what had happened there. Later a different approach was taken, where the names were placed upon the monument to preserve them for another generation.

However, history is given meaning based upon what people do with it. Every year around the date of the execution at the monument at the

## THE MONUMENT AND REFLECTIONS

Meppelerstraatweg there's a memorial service by the schoolchildren, aged 10 to 12, from the primary school de Springplank in Zwolle. In 2019 they were asked what kind of text they would put above the monument if they could design it themselves. They chose the words: 'Don't forget us.' This title has been chosen as the motto of the book.

The reason for it, is that this book also serves as a 'monument'. If the meaning of a 'monument' as given by the Cambridge dictionary is used, then this book could qualify for it, as it serves to honour a past event. Although it's not a work of stone or concrete, it's meant to remember a specific moment in the past. In this book, a group of people has been added, who should also be remembered and weren't visible before: the wives of the men. With this book, their stories are also preserved as much as possible.

History can also be used to create communities, whether real or imagined. In the case of these monuments, several groups of people have been united, that would otherwise have not come in contact with each other. People are connected to the monument for several reasons. The most obvious would be, the ones who have a genealogical connection to it. This includes for instance the descendants or relatives of the men that died. Another group would be people that knew the men that died or those that had a historical connection to them. Such people are, for instance, former members of the Resistance or the people who have experienced the Second World War. An example is Bonno van Dijken, who was a part of 'De Groene' and who attacked the railway bridge to the south of Zwolle, and his wife Clasien de Jong, who was also in the illegal organisation. They felt a connection to the monument and their daughter Petra Crommelin-van Dijken got in touch with me when I was writing this book.

Of course, monuments pass through time and with that passing new connections are made. Currently veterans in Zwolle form one group that are present during memorial services as well as the local primary school that has adopted the monument. The children are educated about the Second World War, human rights, the Holocaust, and the men that died there. Now they too share a link with the monument. As a result, these people from different walks of life, residence, and age, are united in a shared belief and remember that fateful day: 31 March 1945.

The former monument at the Meppelerstraatweg, ca. 1950. (*Sebel family archive*)

A different cross at the Meppelerstraatweg, placed there after the execution, ca. 1945. (*Historisch Centrum Overijssel*)

# THE MONUMENT AND REFLECTIONS

The current monument at the Meppelerstraatweg, date unknown. (*Van Dijk family archive*)

# Endnotes

## Chapter 1: A Horrid Execution

1. Kees Ribbens, *Bewogen jaren: Zwolle in de Tweede Wereldoorlog* (Zwolle, 1995); Marten Roël, *Hotel van Gijtenbeek in de oorlog: Het verzetsleven van J. H. Roël* (z. p., z. j.); Coen Hilbrink e.a, *De Pruus komt: Overijssel in de Tweede Wereldoorlog* (Zwolle, 1990); Wolter Noordman, *De vijftien executies: Liquidaties aan de IJsseloever, april 1945* (Utrecht, 2015).
2. Bert Jan Hartman, *Illegaliteit in Zwolle 1940 – 1945: De effectiviteit van het illegale werk* (Zwolle, 2000) 7-9.

## Chapter 2: The Five Men and Their Families

1. Historisch Centrum Overijssel, Bevolkingsregister 1860 – 1940, Persoonskaart Peter van Dijk, D 123b.
2. The Balistraat was later renamed as the Vechtstraat. Archief Stichting 40-45, file H. M. van Dijk-Verhoeven. Historisch Centrum Overijssel, Bevolkingsregister 1860 – 1940, Persoonskaart Wilhelmus van Dijk, D 122c; Stichting Het Uden-archief van Bressers, persoonskaart Johannes Lambertus Verhoeven, 26 januari 1886.
3. Conversations with Piet van Dijk.
4. Bad Driburg Archiv, Wilhelmus van Dijk, 10.11.1908; Conversations with Piet van Dijk.
5. Nationaal Archief, archief Binnenlandse Strijdkrachten (BS), 2.13.137, inventory number 2399, Dijk, G.A. van (16-7-1901) (Afterwards: NA, BS, 2399).
6. Family archive Van Dijk, letter from Gerrit to Wilhelmus, dated 31 juli 1941.
7. Bad Driburg Archiv, Wilhelmus van Dijk, 10.11.1908.
8. Coen Hilbrink, *De Ondergrondse: Illegaliteit in Overijssel 1940 – 1945* (Den Haag, 1998) 93, 94, 100.

# ENDNOTES

9. NA, BS, 2399; Coen Hilbrink, *De Ondergrondse: Illegaliteit in Overijssel 1940 – 1945* (Den Haag, 1998) 100.
10. Conversations with Piet van Dijk.
11. Conversations with Piet van Dijk; Ministerie van Defensie, Semi-statisch Informatie beheer, Verzetsherdenkingskruis tnv W. A. van Dijk en H. M. van Dijk-Verhoeven.
12. Historisch Centrum Overijssel, woningkaart Balistraat 24. Nationaal Archief, Centraal Archief Bijzondere Rechtspleging, inventory number 74909, Pieter Richard Cieraad (1921) (Afterwards: NA, CABR, 74909).
13. Conversation with Piet van Dijk; conversations with Henk Sattler; Historisch Centrum Overijssel, access number 0726 inventory number 520, Bureau Nationale Veiligheid, Rapporten met verklaringen van diverse personen over personen, zaken en gebeurtenissen, 1945, filenumber 62 (Afterwards: HCO, BNV, 62). Nationaal Archief, Rode Kruis, Centraal Afwikkelingsbureau Duitse Schade-uitkeringen, 2.08.46, Wilhelmus van Dijk, 10/11/1908.
14. Conversations with Henk Sattler.
15. Conversations with Piet van Dijk, 20 april 2018; Historisch Centrum Overijssel, access number 0726 inv. nr. 612, Subcommissie Onderzoek Oorlogsmisdrijven, stukken betreffende onderzoeken naar oorlogsmisdrijven: Zwolle, fusillade 5 personen aan de Meppelerstraatweg op 31 maart 1945 (Afterwards: HCO, SOO, 31/03/1945).
16. National Archives, Records of Headquarters, European Theater of Operations, United States Army (Record Group 498) Entry UD 183 - G-2 Section; Military Intelligence Service; MIS-X Section; Awards Branch; Case Files (Dossiers) Of Dutch Citizens Proposed For Awards For Assisting American Airmen, 1945-47; DIV. 7707th ECIC MIS-X Files – Holland, box 861 Wilhelmus van Dijk. (Afterwards: NA-US, CFODC, Wilhelmus van Dijk).
17. Ribbens, *Bewogen jaren,* 261.
18. NA, BS, 2399; HCO, BNV, 62; Ministerie van Defensie, Semi-statisch Informatie beheer, Verzetsherdenkingskruis tnv W. A. van Dijk en H. M. van Dijk-Verhoeven.
19. HCO, SOO, 31/03/1945.
20. Ribbens, *Bewogen jaren,* 296-297; Ismee Tames, *Doorn in het vlees: foute Nederlanders in de jaren vijftig en zestig* (Amsterdam, 2013) 32.
21. Conversations with Henk Sattler; NA, CABR, 74909.
22. HCO, BNV, 62.
23. HCO, BNV, 62; NA, CABR, 74909.
24. Historisch Centrum Overijssel, access number 0726 inv. nr. 250, Politieke Opsporingsdiensten en Politieke Recherche afdelingen te Zwolle en Kampen,

persoonsdossiers van politiek verdachten, files 194 and 195 (Afterwards: HCO, POD/POR, 194/195).
25. HCO, SOO, 31/03/1945.
26. NA, CABR, 74909.
27. NA, CABR, 74909.
28. Stadsarchief Kampen, persoonskaart Bosch, Hermanus, 1887; Historisch Centrum Leeuwarden, access number 1002 inv. nr. 5018, Persoonskaart Hermanus Bosch.
29. Persoonsdossier Hermanus Bosch, 14.01.05.020, Semi-Statisch InformatieBeheer, Ministerie van Defensie.
30. Gemeente Amsterdam Stadsarchief, persoonskaart Hermanus Bosch; Groninger Archieven, gezinskaarten 1920 – 1939, Hermanus Bosch.
31. Nederlands Instituut voor Militaire Historie, 409 Gevechtsverslagen en -rapporten mei 1940, 517006 Dagboek en verslag van de commandant van het IIIe bataljon van het 25e regiment infanterie majoor A. Floor (Afterwards: NIMH, 409.517006).
32. NIMH, 409.517006.
33. NIMH, 409.517006.
34. Persoonsdossier Hermanus Bosch, 14.01.05.020, Semi-Statisch InformatieBeheer, Ministerie van Defensie; NIMH, 409.517006.
35. Nederlands Instituut voor Oorlogs-, Holocaust- en Genocidestudies, 251a Stichting Landelijke Organisatie voor Hulp aan Onderduikers en Landelijke Knokploegen, 316 Boogaard-Brenk, van (Afterwards NIOD, 251a, 316); conversations with Janny van Hoffen-Bosch; HCO, POD/POR, 194/195.
36. Conversations with Herman Bosch.
37. NIOD, 251a, 316.
38. Conversations with Janny van Hoffen-Bosch.
39. Conversations with Janny van Hoffen-Bosch.
40. Conversations with Janny van Hoffen-Bosch.
41. Conversations with Janny van Hoffen-Bosch.
42. Conversations with Janny van Hoffen-Bosch.
43. Conversations with Janny van Hoffen-Bosch.
44. HCO, SOO, 31/03/1945.
45. HCO, SOO, 31/03/1945.
46. HCO, SOO, 31/03/1945; HCO, BNV, 62.
47. HCO, SOO, 31/03/1945.
48. HCO, BNV, 62.
49. *Het Grote Gebod: Gedenkboek van het verzet in LO en LKP tijdens de Tweede Wereldoorlog* (Kampen, 1989) 399; NIOD, 251a, 316.

## ENDNOTES

50. Henk Westland, 'Malheur in het klooster', *Marechaussee Contact* (2015) 6, 16; Oorlogsdoden Dinkelland, Sebel, Willem, oorlogsdodendinkelland.nl/slachtoffers/oude-gemeente-ootmarsum/sebel-willem/ (geraadpleegd: 9 oktober 2018).
51. Ministerie van Defensie, Semi-Statisch InformatieBeheer, Willem Sebel, 01.04.04.005 (Afterwards: MvD, SSIB, 01.04.04.005).
52. MvD, SSIB, 01.04.04.005.
53. MvD, SSIB, 01.04.04.005.
54. MvD, SSIB, 01.04.04.005.
55. MvD, SSIB, 01.04.04.005; 'jubileum mej. Pot.' *Provinciale Overijsselsche en Zwolsche courant,* 61-11-1934.
56. Gemeentearchief Hardenberg, access number 012, Gemeente Stad Hardenberg, inv. nr. 549, Sebel, W., gemeenteveldwachter.
57. Conversations with Hillie van der Heijden-Sebel; Gemeentearchief Hardenberg, access number 012, Gemeente Stad Hardenberg, inv. nr. 549, Sebel, W., gemeenteveldwachter; 'Burgerlijke stand van Zwolle', *Provinciale Overijsselsche en Zwolsche courant,* 21-11-1935.
58. Conversations with Janny van Hoffen-Bosch.
59. Westland, 'Malheur in het klooster', 16.
60. Westland, 'Malheur in het klooster', 16.
61. Nederlands Instituut voor Oorlogs-, Holocaust- en Genocidestudies 251a Stichting Landelijke Organisatie voor Hulp aan Onderduikers en Landelijke Knokploegen, 340 Salm, v.d.-Sellink (Afterwards: NIOD, 251a, 340).
62. Conversations with Janny van Hoffen-Bosch; conversations with Hillie van der Heijden-Sebel.
63. Conversations with Hillie van der Heijden-Sebel.
64. Westland, 'Malheur in het klooster', 16.
65. Westland, 'Malheur in het klooster', 16-17; Wim Bakker, *Bezetting en verzet: 1940 – 1945 in Meppel en de wijde omgeving* (Meppel, 1984) 56.
66. National Archives, Records of Headquarters, European Theater of Operations, United States Army (Record Group 498) Entry UD 183 – G-2 Section; Military Intelligence Service; MIS-X Section; Awards Branch; Case Files (Dossiers) Of Dutch Citizens Proposed For Awards For Assisting American Airmen, 1945-47; DIV. 7707th ECIC MIS-X Files – Holland, box 834 Willem Sebel (Afterwards: NA, CFOCC, Willem Sebel); Sociale Verzekeringsbank, Afdeling Verzetsdeelnemers en Oorlogsgetroffenen, Willem Sebel (4-4-1901); Nationaal Archief, Rode Kruis, Afwikkelingsbureau Concentratiekampen 2.19.313, Willem Sebel, 4/4/1901.
67. NIOD, 251a, 340.

68. Gerrit de Jonge, 'onderduikbelevenissen van een Lutter jongen', *Rondom den Herdenbergh* (1996) 1, 169-173.
69. HCO, SOO, 31/03/1945.
70. Family archive Alferink.
71. HCO, SOO, 31/03/1945.
72. HCO, SOO, 31/03/1945.
73. Westland, 'Malheur in het klooster', 16-17.
74. HCO, SOO, 31/03/1945.
75. Ministerie van Defensie, Semi-Statisch InformatieBeheer, Persoonsdossier Berend Jan IJzerman, 11.01.14.013 (Afterwards: MvD, SSIB, 11.01.14.013); gesprekken Emmy IJzerman; Familieregister Willem IJzerman en Femmigje Smit, 3 juni 1909; Stadsarchief Kampen, persoonskaart IJzerman, Willem, 1885.
76. MvD, SSIB, 11.01.14.013.
77. Stadsarchief Kampen, access number 00147 inv. nr. 3, Stichting 1940 – 1945, Dossier namen O – IJ; conversations with Emmy IJzerman (Afterwards: SaK, 00147.3).
78. SaK, 00147.3; conversations with Emmy IJzerman; 'vergadering "verzopen dobbertje"', *Kamper nieuwsblad,* 22-09-1945.
79. Conversations with Emmy IJzerman.
80. MvD, SSIB, 11.01.14.013; Nederlands Instituut voor Militaire Historie, 409 Gevechtsverslagen en -rapporten mei 1940, 512034 Verslag van de commandant van de mitrailleurcompagnie van het IIIe bataljon van het 44e regiment infanterie kapitein D. van Hoogstraten. (Afterwards: NIMH, 409.512034).
81. NIMH, 409.512034.
82. NIMH, 409.512034; MvD, SSIB, 11.01.14.013.
83. Conversations with Emmy IJzerman.
84. Conversations with Emmy IJzerman.
85. HCO, SOO, 31/03/1945.
86. HCO, SOO, 31/03/1945.
87. SaK, 00147.3; HCO, SOO, 31/03/1945.
88. HCO, SOO, 31/03/1945.
89. HCO, SOO, 31/03/1945.
90. Stadsarchief Rotterdam, Access number: 494-03 Archief van de Gemeentesecretarie Rotterdam, afdeling Bevolking: bevolkingsboekhouding van Rotterdam en geannexeerde gemeenten, Inventory number: 851-338, Johannes Albertus Muller en Maria van Wingerden, 360492; Stadsarchief Rotterdam, Access number: 494-03 Archief van de Gemeentesecretarie Rotterdam, afdeling Bevolking: bevolkingsboekhouding van Rotterdam en geannexeerde gemeenten, Inventory number: 851-338, Dirk Muller en Elizabeth Toekar, 360139; Family archive Muller.

# ENDNOTES

91. Family archive Muller.
92. Family archive Muller.
93. 'Wedstrijden van "Wilskracht" te Loenen', *De Gooi- en Eemlander*, 4 augustus 1937 en 'Jaarvergadering fanfarecorps', *De Gooi- en Eemlander*, 18 november 1930.
94. 'Loosdrecht, gemeenteraad', *De Gooi- en Eemlander*, 5 augustus 1927.
95. 'Loenen: In een sloot gevallen', *De Gooi- en Eemlander*, 30 juni 1930.
96. 'Loenen: Motorongeval', *De Gooi- en Eemlander*, 29 september 1932.
97. 'Pastoor Brouwer met zijn auto in de Vecht gereden en verdronken', *De Gooi- en Eemlander*, 27 november 1933.
98. 'De onrustbarend hoge Vechtstand', *De Gooi- en Eemlander*, 12 november 1930.
99. 'Onderscheiding sergeant-majoor J. A. Muller', *De Tijd*, 23 oktober 1930 en 'Onderscheiding', *De Gooi- en Eemlander*, 24 oktober 1930.
100. 'De huldiging van het comité van Actie inzake het Vechtgemaal,' *De Gooi- en Eemlander*, 18 januari 1931; 'overdracht van de gedenksteen in het machinegebouw van het Vechtgemaal', *De Gooi- en Eemlander*, 17 januari 1931.
101. 'Politie-Reddingsbrigade voor het Gooi en Utrecht opgericht', *De Gooi- en Eemlander*, 8 mei 1936.
102. 'Nieuwersluis sergeant-majoor J.A. Muller gehuldigd', *De Gooi- en Eemlander*, 19 oktober 1937.
103. Hilbrink, *De Pruus komt*, 13.
104. Nederlands Instituut voor Militaire Historie, 409 Gevechtsverslagen en -rapporten mei 1940, 527009 Verslagen van de commandant van de strategische groep politietroepen Nederweert adjudant onderofficier J.A. Muller (Afterwards: NIMH, 409.527009).
105. NIMH, 409.527009; Nederlands Instituut voor Militaire Historie, 409 Gevechtsverslagen en -rapporten mei 1940, 527010 Verslag van de strategische groep politietroepen Nederweert door sergeant J.M. Geleijns.
106. Nationaal Archief, Ministerie van Defensie: Commandant van het Korps Politietroepen, 2.13.92, 13: Stukken betreffende instructies voor groepen, belast met de bewaking van bruggen in verband met een mogelijke strategische overvalling, alsmede de bezetting en uitrusting van kazematten bij bruggen.
107. NIMH, 409.527009.
108. NIMH, 409.527009.
109. NIMH, 409.527009.
110. NIMH, 409.527009.
111. NIMH, 409.527009.
112. NIMH, 409.527009.
113. NIMH, 409.527009.

114. NIMH, 409.527009.
115. NIMH, 409.527009.
116. NIMH, 409.527009.
117. NIMH, 409.527009.
118. NIMH, 409.527009.
119. Nationaal Archief, Ministerie van Defensie: Commandant van het Korps Politietroepen, 2.13.92, 2: Stukken betreffende de organisatie, samenstelling, personeel en opheffing van de politietroepen (Afterwards: NA, MvD: 2.13.92, 2.)
120. Conversations with Hans Muller.
121. Family archive Muller, 'De Razzia van Rotterdam,' *NIOD,* www.niod.nl/nl/de-razzia-van-rotterdam/razzia-rotterdam (geraadpleegd 30 maart 2019).
122. SaK, 00147.3.
123. HCO, SOO, 31/03/1945.
124. Nationaal Archief, Centraal Archief Bijzondere Rechtspleging, inventory number 108871, Jacob Lijs (1903) (Afterwards: NA, CABR, 108871).
125. Westland, Henk, 'Sportman in het verzet,' *Marechaussee Contact* (2015) 3, 21.
126. NA, CABR, 108871.
127. NA, CABR, 108871.
128. NA, CABR, 108871.
129. NA, CABR, 108871.
130. NA, CABR, 108871.
131. NA, CABR, 108871.
132. NA, CABR, 108871.
133. HCO, SOO, 31/03/1945; NA, CABR, 108871.
134. NA, CABR, 108871.
135. HCO, SOO, 31/03/1945; NA, CABR, 108871.
136. HCO, SOO, 31/03/1945; Conversations with Emmy IJzerman.

## Chapter 3: In the *Huis van Bewaring*

1. Roël, *Hotel van Gijtenbeek in de oorlog,* 50-53, Nationaal Archief, Centraal Archief Bijzondere rechtspleging, inventory number 88312, Nicolaas Polderman (1925) (Shortened: NA, CABR, 88312); Nationaal Archief, Centraal Archief Bijzondere rechtspleging, inventory number 96408, Nicolaas Polderman (1925) (Shortened: NA, CABR, 96408); Nationaal Archief, Centraal Archief Bijzondere rechtspleging, inventory number 70997, Nicolaas Polderman (1925) (Afterwards: NA, CABR, 70997).
2. Roël, *Hotel van Gijtenbeek in de oorlog,* 57.

# ENDNOTES

3. 'Bé Borst had één gebrek: hij was negens bang voor,' 25 maart 1995.
4. Roël, *Hotel van Gijtenbeek in de oorlog,* 50, 57; HCO, SOO, 31/03/1945; Nationaal Archief, Centraal Archief Bijzondere Rechtspleging, inventory number 74093, Hans Kolitz, 1910 (Shortened: NA, CABR, 74093); conversations with Joop Langkamp. In total 20 men were shot, 11 of which came out of Zwolle: J. Albers, H. G. W. Bannink, A. G. Hendriks, A. C. Huiberts (a different Huiberts than the one that received the pilots from Wilhelmus), W. Jakma, E. J. H. Keilholz, J. Langkamp, H. Maaskant, J. H. Roël, J. F. Roskam, S. K. Sietzema, P. Wolfert, H. Kampman, J. Verdriet, J. Seckel, H. W. Jordens, M. A. Boers, B. Dijkman, L. de Wilde, W. Douwsma.
5. NA, CABR, 108871.
6. Ribbens, *Bewogen jaren,* 297.
7. Roël, *Hotel van Gijtenbeek in de oorlog,* 56.
8. *Documentaire Nederland en de Tweede Wereldoorlog, 49: Totale Terreur,* (Zwolle, 1991) 1163; HCO, SOO, 31/03/1945.
9. Nationaal Archief, Centraal Archief Bijzondere Rechtspleging, inventory number 89840, Cornelis Kouwenhoven 1917 (Shortened: NA, CABR, 89840).
10. HCO, SOO, 31/03/1945.
11. NA, CABR, 74093.
12. *Het proces Rauter*, Rijksinstituut voor Oorlogsdocumentatie, Processen 5 ('s-Gravenhage, 1952) 152.
13. NA, CABR, 74093.
14. NA, CABR, 74909.
15. HCO, SOO, 31/03/1945.
16. HCO, SOO, 31/03/1945.
17. NA, CABR, 74909.
18. HCO, SOO, 31/03/1945.
19. HCO, SOO, 31/03/1945.
20. HCO, SOO, 31/03/1945.
21. NA, CABR, 88312; NA, CABR, 96408; NA, CABR, 70997.
22. NA, CABR, 88312, NA, CABR, 74909.
23. HCO, SOO, 31/03/1945; NA, CABR, 88312.
24. HCO, SOO, 31/03/1945.
25. NA, CABR, 108871.
26. HCO, SOO, 31/03/1945; NA, CABR, 108871.
27. HCO, SOO, 31/03/1945.
28. HCO, SOO, 31/03/1945; NA, CABR, 108871.
29. NA, CABR, 108871.
30. NA, CABR, 108871.

## Chapter 4: The Verdict and Westerbork

1. Historisch Centrum Overijssel, access number 0652 inv. nr. 1008, 'Zeewater is zout', ongepubliceerd manuscript over de activiteiten van een verzetsgroep nabij Zwolle in het voorjaar van 1945, door "Karel" (Daan Querner), z.j. [ca. 1980].
2. NA, CABR, 108871.
3. HCO, SOO, 31/03/1945; NA, CABR, 108871.
4. HCO, SOO, 31/03/1945
5. Nationaal Archief, Centraal Archief Bijzondere Rechtspleging, inventory number: 108682. Fritz Martens (1900).
6. HCO, SOO, 31/03/1945; Wim Otterman; *De Stentor*, 'Vijfmaal een nekschot uit wraak', 13 April 2005.
7. Information from the son Jan Jansen about Johannes Hendricus Jansen (1888-1974) (13 March 2019).
8. HCO, SOO, 31/03/1945.
9. HCO, BNV, 62.
10. Roël, *Hotel van Gijtenbeek in de oorlog,* 59.
11. HCO, SOO, 31/03/1945; conversations with Janny van Hoffen-Bosch.
12. Ank Meliesie-Appelhof, 'Herinneringen', *Zwolsch historisch tijdschrift*, 1995, 1, 17.
13. HCO, SOO, 31/03/1945.
14. Historisch Centrum Overijssel, access number 0652 inv. nr.1024, Stichting '40-'45, Documentatie over de koerierster Corrie Kieft uit Zwolle, 1940 – 1995 (Shortened: HCO: DCK).
15. HCO: DCK.
16. HCO: DCK.
17. HCO: DCK.
18. HCO: DCK.
19. Bakker, *Bezetting en verzet,* 170.
20. NA, CABR, 74093.
21. NA, CABR, 74093.
22. NA, CABR, 74093.
23. NA, CABR, 74093.
24. NA, CABR, 74093; Bakker, *Bezetting en verzet,* 171-172.
25. Nationaal Archief, Centraal Archief Bijzondere Rechtspleging, inventory number 87568, Joseph Schreieder (1904) (Afterwards: NA, CABR, 87568).
26. NA, CABR, 74093.
27. NA, CABR, 87568; NA, CABR, 74093.

# ENDNOTES

28. NA, CABR, 87568; NA, CABR, 74093.
29. Bonno van Bellen, *Helden: Het oorlogs-verhaal van twee families* (Sao Paolo, 2017) 89-92.

## Chapter 5: The Aftermath

1. At the Geldersedijk died: John Austin, Gerrit Buunk, Dirk van Diepen, Dirk Eskes, Floris van der Laaken, Gerrit van Unen. At Katerveer died: Sipke Jacob Baarsma, Florimont Beke, Abraham Fros, Aaldert Geerts, R.A. Holvoet, Asse Nijboer, Philip Willem Pander, Egbert Jan Jacob aan het Rot, Folkert Wierda. Joseph Lamarche survived the execution.
2. NA, CABR, 108871.
3. Conversations with Piet van Dijk; conversations with Wim van Dijk.
4. Archief Stichting 40-45, file H. M. van Dijk-Verhoeven.
5. NA, BS, 2399; NA-US, CFODC, Wilhelmus van Dijk; W.J.M. Willemsen, 'Amerikaanse dank voor pilotenhulp', (z.j., z.p.) 10-13.
6. Conversations with Piet van Dijk; conversations with Henk Sattler; gesprekken Anne-Marie van Dijk; Ministerie van Defensie, Semi-statisch Informatie beheer, Verzetsherdenkingskruis tnv W. A. van Dijk en H. M. van Dijk-Verhoeven.
7. *Trouw,* 27 April 1945, 'ter aardebestelling Hermannus [sic] Bosch'; Gesprekken Herman Bosch.
8. NIOD, *De Zwerver,* 5.17. (29 april 1949).
9. Conversations with Janny van Hoffen-Bosch. Trijn and trein = train, sound similar, hence the nickname.
10. Faassen, Dick van, 'Dick van Faassen, oorlogsbeleving van een jongetje uit Lutten', www.tracesofwar.nl/articles/1674/Dick-van-Faassen-oorlogsbeleving-van-een-jongetje-uit-Lutten.htm?c=gw (geraadpleegd, 29 maart 2019); Faassen, G. van, '6 april 1945: een dag van hoop en vrees in Lutten', *Rondom den Herdenbergh: 1940-1945* (1995) 158; Jonge, Gerrit de, 'onderduikbelevenissen van een Lutter jongen', *Rondom den Herdenbergh: 1940-1945* (1995) 169-173.
11. Conversations with Hillie van der Heijden-Sebel; HCO, SOO, 31/03/1945; Oorlogsdoden Dinkelland, Sebel, Willem, oorlogsdodendinkelland.nl/slacht offers/oude-gemeente-o otmarsum/sebel-willem/ (geraadpleegd: 9 oktober 2018); NIOD, 251a, 340. Dodenherdenking = Remembrance of the Dead, every year on 4th May.
12. Ministerie van Defensie, Semi-statisch Informatie beheer, Verzetsherden kingskruis tnv W. Sebel; NA, CFOCC, Willem Sebel.

13. Conversations with Emmy IJzerman.
14. SaK, 00147.3.
15. Ministerie van Defensie, Semi-statisch Informatie beheer, Verzetsherdenking skruis tnv B. J. IJzerman.
16. Stadsarchief Kampen, access number 00147, Stichting 1940-1945, algemeen dossier 1; conversations with Winfried Bij.
17. Conversations with Hans Muller; Westland, 'Sportman in het verzet,' 22.
18. Conversations with Joop Langkamp.
19. HCO, SOO, 31/03/1945.
20. Conversations with Petra Crommelin.
21. HCO, SOO, 31/03/1945; Family archive Alferink.
22. National Archives, War Department. U.S. Forces, European Theater. Military Intelligence Service (MIS). Escape and Evasion Section (MIS-X). Administration Branch. 7/1/1945-3/10/1947, Series: Escape and Evasion Reports, 1942 – 1945, Record Group 498: Records of Headquarters, European Theater of Operations, United States Army (World War II), 1942 – 1947, National Archives Identifier: 5557534, local identifier: E&E 2928, Fuller, Richard P. (2nd LT.).
23. HCO, SOO, 31/03/1945, conversations with Wim Otterman.
24. Information from the son Jan Jansen about Johannes Hendricus Jansen (1888-1974) (13 march 2019).
25. Conversations with Martin Oordijk.

## Chapter 6: Perpetrators and Collaborators

1. Tames, *Doorn in het vlees,* 32 – 36; Wolter Noordman, *De vijftien executies: Liquidaties aan de IJsseloever, april 1945* (Utrecht, 2015)192; Nederlands Instituut voor Oorlogs-, Holocaust- en Genocidestudies, 270a Bijzondere Rechtspleging, 77 Cieraad, D., 22 juni – 5 juli 1947; Nederlands Instituut voor Oorlogs-, Holocaust- en Genocidestudies, KB I Knipselcollectie personen, 1939 Cieraad, P.R.; NA, CABR, 74909; NA, CABR, 74093.
2. NA, CABR, 108871.
3. NA, CABR, 108871.
4. NA, CABR, 108871.
5. A conchi is a sort of free-state.
6. NA, CABR, 108871.
7. *Strijdend Nederland,* 25 augustus 1945, 'Jac. Lijs in de handen van den P.O.D.'; NA, CABR, 108871.

# ENDNOTES

8. NA, CABR, 88312.
9. NA, CABR, 70997.
10. Centraal Bureau Genealogie, persoonskaart Nicolaas Polderman (1925); NA, CABR, 88312.
11. Nationaal Archief, Centraal Archief Bijzondere Rechtspleging, inventory number 74093, Hans Kolitz 1910 (Afterwards: NA, CABR, 74093).
12. Noordman, *De vijftien executies*, 193; Nationaal Archief, Commissies tot Opsporing van Oorlogsmisdadigers, inventory number 1215, Hans Harders (1905). NA, CABR, 74093.
13. Noordman, *De vijftien executies*, 194.
14. Noordman, *De vijftien executies*, 197-198; *Documentaire Nederland en de Tweede Wereldoorlog, 49: Totale Terreur,* (Zwolle, 1991) 1163; HCO, SOO, 31/03/1945.
15. Noordman, *De vijftien executies*, 196-197.
16. Nationaal Archief, Commissies tot Opsporing Oorlogsmisdadigers, inventory number 1130 Walter Bartels (1905); Nationaal Archief, Centraal Archief Bijzondere Rechtspleging, inventory number 393 Walter Bartels (1905).
17. Noordman, *De vijftien executies*, 196. Nationaal Archief, Centraal Archief Bijzondere Rechtspleging, inventory number 286, Fritz Winter (1899).
18. Noordman, *De vijftien executies*, 192. Nationaal Archief, Commissie Opsporing Oorlogsmisdadigers, inventory number 2208, Friedrich Genczyck (1888).
19. Machtergreifung = takeover, *Beamtensauberungsgezetz = law of the removal of officials.* Nationaal Archief, Centraal Archief Bijzondere Rechtspleging, inventory number 108648, Reinhard Stuck (1899); Nationaal Archief, Centraal Archief Bijzondere Rechtspleging, inventory number 86659, Reinhard Stuck (1899).
20. Nationaal Archief, Centraal Archief Bijzondere Rechtspleging, inventory number 112821, Rudolf Schmidt (1899); Nationaal Archief, Centraal Archief Bijzondere Rechtspleging, inventory number 108679, Rudolf Schmidt (1899).
21. NA, CABR, 74093; Nationaal Archief, Centraal Archief Bijzondere Rechtspleging, inventory number 104949, Wilhelm Hukriede (1911), Nationaal Archief, Centraal Archief Bijzondere Rechtspleging, inventory number 108588, Wilhelm Hukriede (1911); Nationaal Archief, Centraal Archief Bijzondere Rechtspleging, inventory number 112818, Wilhelm Hukriede (1911); Nationaal Archief, Centraal Archief Bijzondere Rechtspleging, inventory number 111531, Wilhelm Hukriede (1911).
22. Nationaal Archief, Centraal Archief Bijzondere Rechtspleging, inventarisnumer 112821, Fritz Martens (1900); Nationaal Archief, Commissies tot Opsporing Oorlogsmisdadigers, inventory number 1798, Fritz Martens (1900).

23. Nationaal Archief, Commissies tot Opsporing Oorlogsmisdadigers, inventory number 1432, Willy Mönnich (1905); Nationaal Archief, Centraal Archief Bijzondere Rechtspleging, inventory number 108565, Willy Mönnich (1905).
24. Nationaal Archief, Centraal Archief Bijzondere Rechtspleging, inventory number 104949, Erich Hohmann (1901); Nationaal Archief, Centraal Archief Bijzondere Rechtspleging, inventory number 108667, Erich Hohmann (1901); Nationaal Archief, Centraal Archief Bijzondere Rechtspleging, inventory number 12818 Commissies tot Opsporing Oorlogsmisdadigers, inventory number 2339, Erich Hohmann (1901).

## Chapter 7: The Monument and Reflections

1. Cambridge Dictionary, 'monument', dictionary.cambridge.org/dictionary/english/monument (checked: 2 December 2019).
2. The text in Dutch is: *Hulde aan hen die hier voor ons vielen Zwolle 31 maart 1945. Op deez' droeve plek daar vielen vijf mannen, door Hitler's ploertige knechts. Zij stierven voor ons allen.*
3. Historisch Centrum Overijssel, 0718 dienst openbare werken gemeente Zwolle 280 (Afterwards: HCO, 0718, 280).
4. HCO, 0718, 280.

# Abbreviations

B.d.S.: Befehlshaber der Sicherheitsdienst, commander of the Sicherheitsdienst
Flak: Flugabwehrkanone, a term for German anti-aircraft guns.
LO: Landelijke Organisatie Hulp aan Onderduikers
LKP: Landelijke Knokploegen
OD: Ordedienst
OT: Organisation Todt
SD: Sicherheitsdienst
SiPo: Sicherheitspolizei.

# Bibliography

Bakker, Wim, *Bezetting en verzet: 1940 – 1945 in Meppel en de wijde omgeving* (Meppel, 1984).
Bonno van Bellen, *Helden: Het oorlogsverhaal van twee families* (Sao Paolo, 2017).
*Documentaire Nederland en de Tweede Wereldoorlog, 49: Totale Terreur* (Zwolle, 1991).
*De Gooi- en Eemlander*, 'De huldiging van het comité van Actie inzakte het Vechtgemaal,' 18 January 1931.
*De Gooi- en Eemlander*, 'De onrustbarend hoge Vecht-stand', 12 November 1930.
*De Gooi- en Eemlander*, 'Jaarvergadering fanfarecorps', 18 November 1930.
*De Gooi- en Eemlander*, 'Loenen: In een sloot gevallen', 30 June 1930.
*De Gooi- en Eemlander*, 'Loenen: Motorongeval', 29 September 1932.
*De Gooi- en Eemlander*, 'Loosdrecht, gemeenteraad', 5 August 1927.
*De Gooi- en Eemlander*, 'Nieuwersluis sergeant-majoor J.A. Muller gehuldigd', 19 October 1937.
*De Gooi- en Eemlander*, 'Onderscheiding', 24 October 1930.
*De Gooi- en Eemlander*, 'Overdracht van de gedenksteen in het machinegebouw van het Vechtgemaal', 17 January 1931.
*De Gooi- en Eemlander*, 'Pastoor Brouwer met zijn auto in de Vecht gereden en verdronken', 27 November 1933.
*De Gooi- en Eemlander*, 'Politie-Reddingsbrigade voor het Gooi en Utrecht opgericht', 8 May 1936.
*De Gooi- en Eemlander*, 'Wedstrijden van "Wilskracht" te Loenen', 4 August 1937.
Faassen, Dick van, 'Dick van Faassen, oorlogsbeleving van een jongetje uit Lutten', www.tracesofwar.nl/articles/1674/Dick-van-Faassen-oorlogsbeleving-van-een-jongetje-uit-Lutten.htm?c=gw (Checked: 28 March 2019).

# BIBLIOGRAPHY

Faassen, G. van, '6 april 1945: een dag van hoop en vrees in Lutten', *Rondom den Herdenbergh: 1940-1945* (1995) 156-159.

Hartman, Bert Jan, *Illegaliteit in Zwolle 1940 – 1945: De effectiviteit van het illegale werk* (Zwolle, 2000).

*Het Grote Gebod: Gedenkboek van het verzet in LO en LKP tijdens de Tweede Wereldoorlog* (Kampen, 1989).

*Het proces Rauter*, Rijksinstituut voor Oorlogsdocumentatie, Processen 5 ('s-Gravenhage, 1952).

Hilbrink, Coen et al., *De Pruus komt: Overijssel in de Tweede Wereldoorlog* (Zwolle, 1990).

Hilbrink, Coen, *De Ondergrondse: Illegaliteit in Overijssel 1940 – 1945* (Den Haag, 1998).

Jonge, Gerrit de, 'onderduikbelevenissen van een Lutter jongen', *Rondom den Herdenbergh*: 1940-1945 (1995) 169-173.

Oorlogsdoden Dinkelland, Sebel, Willem, oorlogsdo-dendinkelland.nl/slachtoffers/oude-gemeente-ootmarsum/sebel-willem/(Checked: 9 October 2018).

Meliesie-Appelhof, Ank, 'Herinneringen', *Zwolsch historisch tijdschrift*, 1995, 1, 13-20.

Noordman, Wolter, *De vijftien executies: Liquidaties aan de IJsseloever, april 1945* (Utrecht, 2015).

'De Razzia van Rotterdam,' NIOD, www.niod.nl/nl/de-razzia-van-rotterdam/razzia-rotterdam (Checked 30 March 2019).

Ribbens, Kees, *Bewogen jaren: Zwolle in de Tweede Wereldoorlog* (Zwolle, 1995).

Roël, Marten, *Hotel van Gijtenbeek in de oorlog: Het verzetsleven van J. H. Roël* (z. p., z. j.).

*Strijdend Nederland*, 'Jac. Lijs in de handen van den P.O.D.', 25 August 1945.

*De Stentor*, 'Vijfmaal een nekschot uit wraak', 13 April 2005.

Tames, Ismee, *Doorn in het vlees: foute Nederlanders in de jaren vijftig en zestig* (Amsterdam, 2013).

*De Tijd*, 'Onderscheiding sergeant-majoor J. A. Muller', 23 October 1930.

*Trouw*, 'Teraardebestelling Hermannus [sic] Bosch', 27 April 1945.

Westland, Henk, 'Sportman in het verzet', *Marechaussee Contact* (2015) 3, 20-22.

Westland, Henk, 'Malheur in het klooster'*, Marechaussee Contact* (2015) 6, 16-17.

Willemsen, W.J.M., 'Amerikaanse dank voor piloten-hulp', (z.j., z.p.) 10-13.

# Archives

American Air Museum
Bad Driburg Archiv
Centraal Bureau Genealogie
Familiearchief Alferink
Familiearchief Bosch
Familiearchief IJzerman
Familiearchief Oordijk
Familiearchief Muller
Familiearchief Sebel
Familiearchief Van Dijk
Gemeente Amsterdam Stadarchief
Groninger Archief
Historisch Centrum Leeuwarden
Historisch Centrum Overijssel (HCO)
Ministerie van Defensie (MvD)
Nationaal Archief (NA)
National Archives (NA-GB)
National Archives (NA-US)
Nederlands Instituut voor Oorlogs-, Holocaust- en Geno-cidestudies (NIOD)
Rode Kruis
Sociale Verzekeringsbank
Stadsarchief Kampen (SaK)
Stichting het Uden-archief van Bressers

# Family Sources

Herman Bosch
Albert Bredenhoff
Petra Crommelin
Annemarie van Dijk
Janny van Hoffen-Bosch
Emmy IJzerman
Jan Jansen
Joop Langkamp
Hans Muller
Hillie van der Heijden-Sebel
Henk Sattler
Martin Oordijk
Piet van Dijk
Wil Sebel
Winfried Bij
Wim van Dijk
Wim Otterman

# Index

Alferink, Gerhardus, 30, 32, 55, 65, 67, 96
Apotheker, Frank, 77

Bakker, Laurens, 55, 65, 67
Bannink, Hendrik, 56, 64, 66, 67, 72
Bartels, Walter, 14, 53, 57, 58, 66, 67, 69, 72, 108, 109, 111
Bastiaans, 46
Bramer, Christiaan F., 25, 27
Bramer, Sara, 20, 21
Broekhorst, 93
Beernink, Henk, 7, 12, 13, 20, 22, 29, 55, 57
Berg, Piet van den, 20, 23, 91
Bertus, 92
Beunk, Hendrik, 65
Bijnen, Johannes van, 20
Boer, Jan de, 82, 84
Böll, 74
Boltje, Roelof, 65, 66
Bosch, Gerharda, *see* Peters, Gerharda
Bosch, Herman, 20
Bosch, Hermannus, 15
Bosch, Hermanus, 1, 2, 14, 15, 16, 17, 19, 20, 21, 22, 23, 55, 57, 64, 65, 70, 90, 91, 92, 114
Bosch, Jan, 20
Bosch, Machiel, 20
Broers, Arend, 11
Brouwer, J. J., 40, 41
Brouwer, Thijs, 12, 13, 55, 63, 64, 65, 95
Bruin, Rudolf de, 27

Cieraad, Piet R., 12, 13, 14, 22, 53, 57, 58, 63, 64, 67, 69, 74, 76, 95, 98, 99

Detand, Helmuth, 84
Diele, Hendrik, 64
Dijk, Gerrit A. van, 6, 7, 9, 10, 12, 13, 23, 64, 89
Dijk, Hendrica van, *see* Hendrica Verhoeven
Dijk, Frans van, 6, 8
Dijk, Peter van (1913-1987), 6, 7, 8, 12, 89
Dijk, Peter van (1876-1971), 5
Dijk, Piet van (1936-1966), 6, 88
Dijk, Piet van (1927), 10, 89
Dijk, Jan van, 6, 88
Dijk, Joke van, 6, 89
Dijk, Wim van, 6
Dijk, Wilhelmus. A. M. van, 1, 2, 5, 6, 7, 8, 9, 10, 11, 12, 13, 14, 25, 55, 56, 57, 63, 64, 65, 70, 74, 76, 77, 78, 95, 114
Dijken, Bonno van, 85, 96, 115
Dorp, Maria van, 23
Douwes, Guillette, 57
Drosten, K. A., 29

Eisenjower, Dwigt D., 89
Essen, Sienna van, 81
Ester, Joop, 63

Fuller, Richard, 10, 11, 96

# INDEX

Galle, Americo S., 108
Geigolath, Hugo, 82, 84
Geleijns, 46
Genczyk, Friedrich, 73, 109
Gort, Albert, 51, 52, 53, 100
Grams, Sonja, 111
Graver, Jan de, 11

Habing, Jo, 82
Hamming, Lammert, 78
Hanekamp, Gerritdina, 33, 36, 37, 67, 68, 93, 94
Hartholt, Hendrik, 81, 82, 84
Heins, J. T., 48
Hitler, Adolf, 43, 61
Himmler, Heinrich, 58
Hoeven, v. d., 40
Hohmann, Erich, 76, 112
Hoogstraten, David van, 35
Horst, Andries van der, 75
Horst, Dini van der, 75
Houwert, 30, 32
Huiberts, Albertus, 11
Huizing, 81
Hukriede, Wilhelm, 74, 110, 111
Hurk, C. J., 29

Ingenhoes, 41
IJzerman, Berend J. 1, 2, 32, 33, 34, 35, 36, 37, 49, 52, 53, 54, 55, 57, 67, 70, 72, 73, 93, 94, 95, 100, 111, 114
IJzerman, Emmy, 33, 34, 35, 93
IJzerman, Gerritdina, *see* Hanekamp, Gerritdina
IJzerman, Willem 32

Jäger-Wolhoff, Emelie, 37, 49, 52, 53, 54, 67, 68, 69, 78, 79
Jansen, Johannes, 74, 75, 96
Jonge, Gerrit de, 29
Jong, Clasien de, 96, 115

Kamp, Huub van der, 92
Kamphuis, Jan, 75

Kamphuis, Trijntje, 92
Keers, 98
Klerk, de, 55, 65
Kolitz, Hans, 59, 60, 61, 82, 84, 85, 106, 107
Knickmeijer, 84
Knipmeijer, 70
Krachting, 40
Kreder, Arend, 74
Kuik, 30, 32

Laber, 106
Langkamp, Johan, 56, 57, 65, 66, 67, 72, 95, 96, 105
Leeuw, de, 40
LeLoux, Gerhardus, 14
Lettinck, 104
Lont, Dirk, 65
Linden, v. d., 40
Lippe Biesterfeld, Bernhard of, 16
Lijs, Jacob, 50, 51, 52, 53, 54, 57, 68, 69, 70, 99, 100, 105
Lucas, 99

Major, Leo, 87
Manders, Egbertus, 88
Marlowe, Joe, 10, 11
Martens, Fritz, 51, 53, 57, 67, 68, 69, 72, 73, 93, 111
Maurik, van, 44, 45, 46, 47
Meliesie-Appelhof, Ank, 77
Mensink, J. H., 29
Mensink, Willemien, 25, 28
Meijer, Cornelis, 82, 84
Meijer, Herman, 22, 63
Meyer-Noach, 10
Mönnich, Willy, 22, 53, 57, 58, 111
Muller, Bep, 38, 69, 94
Muller, Johannes A., 1, 2, 36, 37, 38, 39, 40, 41, 42, 43, 44, 45, 46, 47, 48, 49, 53, 54, 55, 57, 67, 68, 69, 70, 72, 73, 93, 94, 95, 100, 111, 114
Muller, Joop, 38, 48, 49, 69, 94
Muller, Maria, *see* Wingerden, Maria van

Munnik, 90
Mussert, Anton, 12, 42

Neijboom, 14
Nijenhuis, Berend, 82, 84

Oberman, Piet, 20, 23
Oom Willem, 29
Oordijk, Heimert, 75, 77, 96
Oorschot, Johannes van, 27
Otterman, Harm-Jan, 74, 96
Otterman, Wim, 75, 96
Oude Hilbrink, 40
Overbeek, Frederik, 27

Peer, Pite, 29
Peters, Gerharda, 17, 19, 22, 23, 65, 90
Plezier, Aaltje, 84
Pieterman, Harm, 65
Polderman, Nicolaas, 55, 65, 66, 67, 96, 105, 106
Posthuma, L. L., 40, 41
Pot-Naarding, 25

Querner, Daan, 72

Rauch, Joseph, 51, 53, 54, 59, 62, 63, 69, 108
Rauter, Hanns, 58, 59, 108
Roëll, Theo, 65
Ridder of Rappard, Ernst H., 50
Rijn, van, 30

Sandberg, Edward, 50, 52
Sattler, 9, 13
Sattler, Aeldert, 9, 78, 89
Sattler, Hendrik, 9
Schmidt, Rudolf, 75, 110
Schöngarth, Karl, 58, 59, 61, 82, 85, 106, 108
Schothorst, E. van, 100
Schrader, Anton, 107
Schreieder, Joseph, 107
Schulte Nordholt, Jan Willem, 21
Schuurman, H., 29

Sebel, Gerrit, 23
Sebel, Willem, 1, 2, 23, 24, 25, 27, 28, 29, 30, 32, 55, 57, 65, 66, 67, 70, 74, 78, 92, 93, 96, 105, 114
Sebel, Willemien, *see* Mensink, Willemien
Selhorst, Hendrik, 74
Selles, Hilligje, 15
Seyss-Inquart, 27
Smit, 39
Smit, Femmigje, 32
Spijkerman, Hendrik, 66, 105
Sportel, A., 27, 29
Steemers, 44, 45, 46, 47
Stomp, Johan, 81, 82, 84
Stuck, Reinhard, 22, 74, 109, 110
Swinderen, Q. J., 42

Tardi, Casperus, 74, 75, 96
Tempelman, Hendrika, 56, 67, 95
Thijs, 90
Thümmel, Paul, 80, 81, 82, 84

Uiterwijk, 80

Verheul, 96
Vermeulen, 41, 42
Verhoeven, Arnoldus, 9
Verhoeven, Hendrica, 5, 6, 7, 8, 10, 12, 13, 63, 64, 76, 78, 79, 88, 89
Verhoeven, Theodora, 9
Vries, de, 40

Wiemers, 29
Wierike, Maria te, 5
Winter, Fritz, 73, 74, 76, 77, 109
Wingerden, Maria H. van, 38, 69, 70, 78, 79, 94
Winkelman, Henri, 16, 17

Zeehandelaar, Henny, 56, 57
Zeehandelaar, Henriëtte, 57
Zeehandelaar, Regina, 57
Zilverberg, 8